In the Guts Of Health Care

The case for universal health care coverage through a single payer system

by

Fouad B. Michael, M.D.

authorHOUSE®

AuthorHouse™
1663 Liberty Drive
Bloomington, IN 47403
www.authorhouse.com
Phone: 1-800-839-8640

*This book is a work of non-fiction. Unless otherwise noted, the author
and the publisher make no explicit guarantees as to the accuracy of
the information contained in this book and in some cases, names of
people and places have been altered to protect their privacy.*

First published by AuthorHouse 3/3/2010

ISBN: 978-1-4184-6474-5 (sc)

Printed in the United States of America
Bloomington, Indiana

This book is printed on acid-free paper.

Contents

Preface

I intend in this book to share with you my own experience as a practicing physician in an attempt to shed some light on the difficult subject of health care reform that challenged our imagination for decades. I bring with me personal knowledge of different health care systems as I grew up and worked in a socialist country with its own idiosyncrasies then immigrated and worked in the United States where different rules determined how health care is delivered.

My passion for health care reform started when I was in medical school in a country where poverty, ignorance and limited resources made it difficult for the doctor to give, and the patient to receive, the proper health care. This passion increased in my adopted country as I felt the pain of my patients and confronted their fears and hopes which brought back my own believes that every patient should receive the proper care that his condition requires, and that the primary duty of the doctor is to care for his patients' needs, not just to make money. I saw the reverse happening in the fee-for-service system, which invited abusive behavior from doctors and patients alike and produced the unconscionable escalation of the cost of health care. As a consequence, we became victims to the more abusive system of HMO's and managed care, which were supposed to control the cost and improve the quality of health care but they ultimately and inherently accomplished the opposite.

You have to be in the guts of health care to know its complexities. You might need to arm yourself with insights into the plethora of disciplines that are required to navigate through its intricate convolutions. You might need, at the same time, to be a doctor, a patient, a hospital administrator, a lawyer, a pharmaceutical executive, a judge and a politician to understand what's going on. However, just being a human being is all that you need to find your way.

I do not claim to be all of the above; no one can. But at least I am a physician and a patient myself and I have certainly dealt, like some of you, with all the other players who have a say in what we call health care. I fought my battles with the government, the health care insurance companies, the medical establishment, the legal system, and the ups and downs of a long career and became convinced of the need for a final resolution to a clearly defective system. It is enough to know that more than forty million people in our country are without health insurance, that an equal number is underinsured, that a large number of our children are not immunized and that some of our senior citizens have to choose between filling their prescriptions or buying food to make you see the need for a definitive health care reform instead of the patch work that we have been doing in previous attempts and in the current, so called, reform.

I bring with me the contrast of a different culture, basic and spiritual, but certainly as human as our own. I bring with me the lessons I learned from my teaching years and my daily rounds in the sacred corridors of medicine. I bring with me all the baggage and I'll spread it in front of your critical eyes that you might see and think and, hopefully, find your way through the complex world of health care.

This book is not an autobiographical narrative about me though it might seem as such in some instances. It is in fact about you who actually supplied the stories, the inspiration and the human dimension when you walked into my office and touched my mind and my soul and made me determined to look for a simple, manageable and cost effective way to deliver care to our patients.

I intend to take you in this book on a journey through the guts of health care, and I promise to tell you the whole truth as I saw it. I'll hide nothing, not the nutritious juices nor the filthy refuse. So, let's start our journey.

Prologue

In less than six years, I accomplished my American dream: a new house, a new practice in my medical field, a manageable debt, and a healthy family. It was July 1st. 1974

On second thought, it wasn't only six years - it was 37 years, thirty of which were the formative years in Egypt where I grew up and studied to become a medical doctor. They should be included in the count toward my American dream.

I was born in the holy land when it was called Palestine. (It is now Israel.) Did the place of my birth matter to me? Yes and no. Yes it mattered during one of my trips to Egypt when the emigration officer in Cairo Airport questioned me about my national origin because my American passport stated that I was born in Israel. When I answered that I was originally of Egyptian descent, born to Egyptian parents in what is now

Israel, he sarcastically noted that there was no Israel in 1937. Thankfully, no further historical lessons were enunciated, and he let me through.

But no, it never mattered to me in the least. I have always thought of myself as Egyptian by genes, Palestinian by birth, Jewish by common distant ancestors, Muslim by proximity, Coptic Christian by faith, and American by choice – in short, a human being as genuine as all of the above and more. And that's why I came to America - it was the universal human culture I absorbed growing up in Egypt and the yearning for the American dream of "life, liberty and the pursuit of happiness" that made me come to America.

I tried to go to America at a younger age when I asked my father to allow me to have a stateless passport that would have made it easy for me to leave Egypt, but he refused. "You mustn't give up your Egyptian nationality," he said. I had to wait until adulthood to emigrate. Thankfully, I used those years to learn more about humanity's evolutionary drive and everything I could about America. By the time I finished medical school, I was completely americanized. I was ready to go.

However, this couldn't be done immediately. By then, Nasser was the ruler of Egypt, and he became the new Pharaoh who refused to let his people go - college graduates were not allowed to leave the country and all medical graduates were required to serve for two years in the public health care system.

After a year of internship at Cairo University Hospitals, I was sent to serve in a remote village in Southern Egypt. I welcomed the opportunity with the enthusiasm of the young and the beliefs of the idealist. However, I was drafted in the army after serving there for only six months, and I had to leave the public health care sector.

I spent three months in the military academy then graduated as a second lieutenant in the medical corps. I subsequently served in Yemen, returned to the public health care system, was recalled and served in the army during the '67 war, returned to the public health care sector after the end of that war, and was finally freed and allowed to go.

I experienced firsthand the Egyptian socialist revolution of the sixties and lived through all the global transformations during those tumultuous years. Above all, I studied and served in a national health care system with all its flaws and ambitions. That's where I found out what it means for patient's to be poor and sick, and for doctors to be helpers and healers. My first assignment was in a rural collective unit, which served the farmers' needs in agriculture, animal husbandry, social programs, and health care. My medical unit consisted of eight inpatient beds, a small ill-equipped operating room, an outpatient clinic, and a meagerly supplied pharmacy. I saw about a hundred patients a day without any ancillary help: no X ray, no laboratory and very few drugs.

Doctors were given extra pay to compensate them for this full-time job. In return, they were forbidden to charge the patients for their services. However, most of the doctors ignored the law; they continued to have private practices on the side. I couldn't allow myself to do the same as I believed in the fairness of the system, the obligation to lessen patients' suffering, and the immorality of making more money on the expense of the poor.

A stethoscope and a blood pressure apparatus were my only helping tools. My guiding tools, though, were my sight, my hearing, my touch, and an honest desire to help.

I was properly trained in that regard at my medical school and during the internship year. We were taught to depend on our clinical sense. Even with the availability of some basic technological help, we would had been reprimanded by our seniors if the X ray or cardiogram or laboratory tests we ordered came back as normal or showed some abnormalities we didn't foresee beforehand. Our clinical training required us to listen to the patient, examine him/her thoroughly and make a judgment with the minimum resources we had. All of that served me well during my work in that remote rural center.

In America, I repeated the internship and the residency training as is required of all foreign graduates, and was ultimately certified by the American Board of Medical Specialties as an Otolaryngologist. I then started my own private practice in a suburb of a big city on July 1st. 1974.

It turned out that my clinical training in a poor country served me equally as well in the richest country in the world with all its sophisticated technology. However, the shock of the new didn't distract me from the basic responsibility of caring for the sick with proper judgment, humane touch and with the least expense.

The respect for the patient as a fellow human being stayed with me throughout my career in America. This made me more conscious, and more critical, of what was unfolding in our health care system.

I kept a teaching position at the hospital where I did my residency training. I shortly gained an award for teaching excellence. In less than five years, I was appointed as chief of my department in the hospital where I performed most of my work. All that gave me an insider's look at our medical education and the way hospitals function and doctors behave. Ultimately, I also had my share of malpractice suits, which gave me a learning experience of our legal system

Over the years, my interest in health care reform developed in hand with my own experience. That's why I ultimately retired from the practice of medicine at the young age of 62 to study this subject and tell my own story. Having worked in two different political systems has given me an advantage in this regard. In Egypt, I saw the defects of a dictatorship, no matter what good intentions it claimed. In America, I enjoyed the wonders of a democratic system and I learned not to fear a democratic government and to trust the wisdom of the people who are in control of their government.

In the 1992, 2000 and 2004 presidential campaigns, health care reform was one of the big political issues with no resolution insight. One more time, in the 2008 campaign, when the escalating cost became prohibitive, the obscene numbers of the uninsured and the underinsured reached untold millions, and the strain on our economy was too obvious to be ignored any longer, health care reform became an urgent political issue no less than our weariness from two unresolved wars and our apprehension from an approaching economic meltdown. Finally, a meaningful reform was in sight. Unfortunately, president Obama squandered his political capital from a victorious landslide mandate and took a behind-the-scene role that permitted our congressional geniuses to endlessly debate an issue that needed no further debate and formulate a vertiginous bill of a few thousand pages that will ultimately benefit the insurance companies and the other parasites that have corrupted our banks and our health to begin with. Patching and nibbling at the edges will not work. We have to remember what happened in 1993-1994 when Hillary Clinton and her commission came up with a not-too-much different plan that's equally complicated - it similarly required thousands of pages to spell it out. History repeated itself, yet this time around a defective congressional plan was enacted into law. There is no doubt that, even with this plan, we are bound to face the same problems again and again.

My American dream, and yours, would not be complete without a simple, comprehensive, equitable, and cost effective health care system that can take care of our health needs without bankrupting our economy. Hard working individuals of healthy minds and bodies generate our wealth. Human beings make the machines and not vise versa. The logic is clear: if we maintained the health of our people, they would generate all the wealth that's possible.

With this said, let's find our way towards the missing but necessary complement to a more perfect American dream.

In the Beginning

In the early seventies, it wasn't that difficult to start a medical practice: all you had to do was rent an office space, hang your shingles and cover a manageable overhead. It was even less difficult in my case, thanks to the generosity of friends and a healthy dose of good luck.

I developed a few friendships during my residency that contributed favorably to my future life. A colleague of mine, who graduated a few years earlier, established a successful practice in a suburb of the big city. He subsequently decided to relocate in another state and offered me his practice. "For how much?" I asked. "For nothing," he answered. And the deal was done.

My wife and I thought it better for us to buy a house close to the practice, but we didn't have enough money for the down payment. "Buy it," said the chief of my residency program. When I told him that we didn't have enough money, he offered to lend it to me without interest. "But why?" I asked. "Just be a good boy and do a good job," he explained. We bought the house.

I asked my Jewish lawyer for his bill after we had signed the contract for a house. "No charge," he said. "You remind me of myself when I was starting my career." This was his explanation for this unexpected generosity. He finally accepted much less than the customary fees at that time.

I discovered that people were the same no matter where they lived on this wonderful planet. My American friends reminded me of the compassionate people I served in that little village in the south of Egypt. I especially remember the Omda (mayor) of that little village who didn't even read or write, but he had the wisdom of a few thousand years in his heart. I remember him as he approached me to borrow 20 pounds when I was just starting my work in his little village. At that time, the Egyptian pound was equal to a dollar, and the twenty pounds were the total of my salary for a month. I happily gave him the money. Before I left for the service, he returned those twenty pounds to me. When I asked him to keep them, he confessed that he didn't need them to begin with. He only wanted to save them for me in case I needed them in the future. My American friends did even better than that; they gave me their own money.

I subleased a space in one of the prestigious medical buildings in the area. Jews and blacks were not welcomed there, but, paradoxically, a foreigner like me was! This was my first experience with the prevailing prejudice at that time. Thankfully, the majority of doctors in that building are now Jews, blacks and foreigners. More similar experiences followed.

One of the patients I saw early in my new practice was under the care of the previous doctor who had operated on him for cancer of the sinuses in the same hospital where I was a resident. It happened that I participated in that surgery and cared for that patient during his hospitalization. Subsequently we became good friends.

The first time I saw him in my new office, he confided to me that his primary care physician wanted him to be followed up by another doctor. "No foreign doctor is going to take care of you," his physician had told him. The patient still came to me. He warned that I would meet more bigotry like that, but he reassured me by saying, "Just do a good job and everything will be just fine." I tried to do exactly that during the following 25 years, and it paid off. This was the America I dreamed of. Truly, money doesn't grow on trees, but it is there for those who are willing to work for it.

With hard work and more good luck, I ultimately built a good practice. Although I encountered difficulties in supporting my family in the beginning and confronted abusive behavior from both doctors and patients,

I kept my sanity all through, drawing on the blessings of this great country that accepted me as a citizen and allowed me to exercise my freedom to practice the profession I loved.

At the same time, I couldn't forget the poor and the needy patients of the old country who taught me the respect for the infirm and the obligation to lessen the suffering regardless of any monetary reward. During the following 25 years, I witnessed the gradual change of a mostly not-for-profit system into an overwhelmingly for-profit one. I also saw the destructive power of advertisement, the defects of our legal system and the abuses that drained our health budget.

I became especially disillusioned with the gradual change of the medical practice from a profession to a business, which became more dramatized, and sadly encouraged, in the continuing medical education courses every doctor was required to take. One of those courses I attended was dedicated to the justification of making a business out of medical practice and the new ethics of survival. I knew then that we were heading in the wrong direction, and I refused to follow the herd.

At the same time, I became involved in the endless debate about the need for the reform that doesn't happen. I wrote letters to Senator Edward Kennedy who, or more correctly one of his staff, reassured me about his commitment to health care reform, but I sensed that he wasn't too optimistic about the prospect of that reform. I kept writing to the local newspapers and the medical journals without receiving a response most of the time and with discouraging responses in other times. Yet, I kept my faith that some day this great country would do the right thing for our patients.

In this book, I plan to expose what I know to be the seeds of corruption that inflict serious damage on our health care system and drain billions of dollars that should be properly spent on the care of our sick people. At the same time, I'll try to address the legitimate as well as the illegitimate concerns of opponents to any meaningful health care reform.

The following story is as good as any to start with and to illustrate some of the problems we have to deal with.

An older colleague of mine asked me to see one of his patients whom he admitted to the hospital for a swallowing problem. He diagnosed him with Zenker's Diverticulum, (a pouch or hernia from the upper esophagus, the food passage,) and he wanted me to evaluate the patient and assist in his coming surgery.

I went to the radiology department to review the barium study and the CT scan that were already done. True, the barium study showed a large diverticulum compressing and obstructing the esophagus. But to my surprise, the scan showed a tumor of the larynx, (Voice box.) My understanding was that the patient was treated a year earlier for cancer of the larynx with radiation, and his doctor had told me that the scan was negative. The changes I saw on the scan, I surmised, could have been due to the effects of radiation. But I decided to personally examine the patient.

I found the patient to be a sixty years old man. Life-long smoking irreparably damaged his lungs. The result was Chronic Obstructive Pulmonary Disease (COPD) - a fancy name for "emphysema." The bronchial tubes had lost their rigidity and became obstructed by secretions that could not be cleared by its damaged and inefficient lining membranes. The lungs were not spongy anymore. They had lost their elastic framework and their resilience, and had become shredded like a worn-out piece of rag. The rib cage ballooned to a barrel-shape skeleton from long standing overwork to fill the lungs with air. (You find all these signs, or what we call physical findings, by looking, feeling, tapping with your fingers and listening with your stethoscope.)

Chronic Obstructive Pulmonary Disease was the original problem. The cancer came later. On top of that, he had lost 50 pounds in just three months.

When I examined the patient, I surely found the cancer that the scan had suggested. I knew right then that his proper treatment should be total laryngectomy (removal of the voice box), which should, in all probability, cure his cancer and easily resect the diverticulum at the same time. I discussed all my findings and recommendations with his doctor. He wanted me to take over the care of that patient.

I sat down with the patient and his wife and explained my findings and recommendation to them. At the end, I asked for permission to do a biopsy and remove the voice box if the biopsy was positive for cancer.

"This is not our understanding," the wife said as she assumed the role of the spokes-person. "We were told that the cancer was cured and that the scan was negative," she added.

I sensed the resentment and the anger in her voice, and I realized that it wasn't going to be easy. "I hope that you're right," I reassuringly said. "The biopsy will tell us what it is. My duty is to tell you the truth as I see it, and this is the truth."

"Can't you just fix this diverticulum and make him swallow?" She asked.

"Yes we can do that," I diplomatically said, "but this is not the right decision. To remove the diverticulum, we have to make a long incision in the neck, open the esophagus and repair it, and then feed him through a tube down his nose for about one week. We have to do the same if we remove the voice box. Yes he will lose his voice, but we can teach him to talk in a different way. The cure rate is excellent and he can manage very well like all other patients who had the same surgery," I explained.

She interrupted me with the same angry voice. "The other doctor didn't explain all that to us. What you are telling us now is very shocking and we need time to think about it."

I thought it was prudent to leave it at that. They got the message and they would make the right decision. In the meantime, I asked their permission to insert a central line (a catheter in the big vein of the neck) to give him intravenous nutrition until they decided about the surgery. They consented to the insertion of the catheter and I asked the resident to do it.

I was in my office when the resident called me with the bad news that he had punctured the lung and produced a pneumothorax (air in the chest cavity) while he was inserting the intravenous catheter. I called a chest surgeon who inserted a chest tube to drain the air from the chest and allow the lung to re-expand.

I saw the patient later that day. He greeted me by saying in a hoarse voice, "now I can sue you, doctor." I pretended that I didn't hear what he had just said; malpractice wasn't on my mind, though I didn't dismiss it completely. I was worried more about his well being and his reluctance to consent to the proper surgery for his condition. I listened to his lungs and checked the chest tube. I was satisfied that everything was proper, and I left.

The chest tube was removed after a few days and we went back to the waiting game. They couldn't make up their minds about the surgery. However, a succession of events followed that made the question of surgery irrelevant.

He soon developed pneumonia from aspiration due to his swallowing difficulty and his incompetent larynx. This was followed by respiratory failure that required intubation. He ended in the ICU (Intensive Care Unit) and on a respirator. Kidney failure came next and he was started on dialysis. He expired 3 months later, but not before the loss of countless work-force hours and a huge expense.

My colleague in this story represents a sizable number of doctors who are either incompetent, abusive or of advanced age to properly perform delicate surgeries but not willing to quit the practice of medicine. He reminded me of another doctor who was one of my attendings when I was a resident. That attending was over seventy years old with a huge ENT practice in the big city. He used to admit his surgical patients to the hospital, but he wasn't capable of doing the surgery. He used us, his residents, to do the surgeries for him. We got the experience, and he made the money.

The patient I described here was a good man, but he abused his body by unhealthy habits. However, he resented the truth when he became

9

sick, and he only wanted a magic bullet to cure his problem. He was also fantasizing about winning a malpractice lottery, though he might not have been able to act on his fantasies. His journey to his death raises a lot of questions about how we are dealing with the dying process and the care for the terminally ill that consume a large portion of our health care dollars in the last few months of our lives.

I have a lot of explaining to do in the next few chapters. So let me take you through the guts of our health care system.

Doctors are not Immune from Greed

It wasn't easy for me to write this chapter. I have to stress up front that our doctors are truly the best in the world. The few bad apples I am talking about here represent only the rare doctors who disproportionately tarnish the image of the rest of us. Yet, the harm they inflict should be understood and managed in order to give our patients the best care with the least affordable cost possible. As I intend to present our health care system as it actually exists and as I see it, I find it necessary to include a chapter like this one to bring to light one of the issues we have to deal with even if, in doing so, some readers might reach unintended conclusions. So, let me be clear: The best medical care, (not health care as I'll explain later) in the world that our citizens, some but certainly not all, enjoy became possible through the hard work of the honorable and competent doctors we have. With this clarification, I feel more comfortable to return to my narration.

One day, I received a call from a surgeon who was in the ICU caring for a trauma patient. He was angry because one of my ENT staff refused to come and see his patient.

A Cricothyrotomy (a quick form of an urgent tracheostomy) was performed on that patient when he was initially brought to the emergency room. The surgeon wanted to change that to a formal tracheostomy, as was usually done. He judged that an ENT surgeon was better qualified to do it than himself, and that's why he called the ENT specialist on call.

I volunteered to do the surgery and promised to investigate the whole incident after that.

The ICU head nurse was waiting for me when I arrived. She informed me that this particular ENT specialist was notorious for refusing to see patients if they happened not to have medical insurance. When he knew that this patient didn't have insurance, she explained, he refused to come.

I performed the required tracheostomy then called that ENT doctor.

He claimed that he was busy in his office and couldn't possibly leave a load of patients there to come and do the required tracheostomy. When I told him that he could have come after his office hours, being that this surgery was not necessarily urgent, he flatly said that he was "in the market to make money" (Yes, those were his exact words,) and that this patient had no insurance.

I reminded him that his primary concern should be caring for the patients. Moreover, when a colleague asks for help, medical ethics and proper standards of honor require a positive response regardless of the monetary issues. He must have sensed my anger and my determination to hold him accountable for his behavior. Next day, he submitted his resignation from that hospital. He thus saved himself from a definite review and a disciplinary action from the executive board of the medical staff as I had indicated to him. Unfortunately, I was also sure that he would exercise his money-making goal somewhere else.

In today's world, most of the medical seminars, courses and meetings invariably include a lecture or at least a discussion on how to bill and on how to ensure payments for one's fees. Non-medical entrepreneurs joined in this "educational" service with relentless advertisement that guaranteed doubling or tripling of one's income. The following stories illustrate the cost we pay for, and the harm we receive from, these educational services.

A doctor I knew used to say, "You have to maximize your income by any means possible." His means included over-coding and unbundling. In the case of over-coding, he would bill for a higher service code to get higher reimbursement, and in the case of the unbundling, he would innumerate different steps of one operation as separate components and bill for each component as a separate operation. True, the insurance companies ultimately caught up with these coding abuses but not before my friend and many more like him became adept at using modifiers and other 'creative' billing techniques. They were always one step ahead in this cat and mouse game. The "educational courses" they attended showed them how to make their money and maximize their income.

I encountered another young doctor who proudly told me that he made over a million-dollar income in his first year of practice. I asked him about the secret of his success when I never dreamed of making that much in 20 years. He didn't hesitate to tell me about his innovative billing techniques. Unbundling was one of his tools. At that time, "FESS" (Functional Endoscopic Sinus Surgery) was coming into vogue in the ENT field. The procedure entails operating on the four paired sinuses under the guidance of a scope, thus its name. This enterprising doctor was unbundling this one operation into its 8 components and billing $14,000-16,000 for it. (The total operation shouldn't take more than one hour to perform.) He reasoned that the insurance companies were screwing us, so why not screw them in return!

One day, a nurse brought to my office her teenage son for possible tonsillectomy. He was getting frequent tonsillar infections that required several antibiotics and caused him to lose too many school days. My evaluation showed markedly diseased and obstructive tonsils, and I was convinced that he would benefit from the surgery. The mother accepted my judgment and was already prepared for my recommendation. When we reviewed her medical insurance policy, we found out that a second opinion was required. She promised to seek the second opinion and get back to me.

She called back in a few days saying that the second-opinion doctor agreed on the surgery. However, he accidentally found fluid in one of her son's ears and put him on antibiotics for it, though her son never complained of any ear pain or hearing loss. I told her to bring him back so I could evaluate him myself and do something about this ear fluid during his coming tonsillectomy, if that was needed.

When I saw him in my office for the second time, his ears were perfectly normal. There was no evidence of any fluid in either ear and I didn't need any tests to confirm my findings. The mother reassured me that she wasn't worried about his ears. Then, she volunteered that the second opinion doctor had performed a hearing test and a tympanogram (a test to measure the pressure in the middle ear), which were normal. He also examined him with a telescope through the nose. When I asked her if all that was necessary, she sarcastically said that she didn't think so. "I know exactly why he did all these test: money," she said.

I knew that too. Sadly enough, that doctor must have cost us close to $1000 for his second opinion and the unnecessary tests. I guess that he was following the recipe he must have learned from one of those courses. The truth of the matter is that, too often, profit is the driving force behind the indications, or lack of them, in performing or not performing procedures or even surgery. And the change that transformed medicine into a business gave us the needed justification. (More on that later.)

A neighboring doctor used to do a lot of tonsillectomies when the insurance companies paid over $2000 for the surgery. His indications for this operation decreased when the reimbursement was reduced to less than $300 and completely disappeared when it reached $60. He reasoned that going to the operating room and assuming the risk of complications for this little money didn't warrant his trouble. He also reasoned that he could use his time more profitably by staying in his office and seeing more patients than going to the O.R.

The worst case of greed, even outright fraud, I encountered happened with an orthopedic doctor I knew. (I am not trying here to single out this specialty, but I can assure you that this example is not completely unknown in the other specialties.)

During a medical meeting I was attending, the beeper of a doctor, an orthopedist friend of mine sitting next to me, went off. The message was coming from the emergency room. He wanted to finish the meeting before he would answer that call.

I went to the E.R. with him. We found that the patient had expired by the time we reached there. This didn't stop my orthopedic friend from writing a consultation note on the dead man's chart and dictating an operative report for reduction of a fracture he never performed.

When I reminded him that the patient was dead before our arrival, he unabashedly said that the patient had good insurance, and that they would pay for the services he was billing for. And why not, he reasoned, didn't he give the time and effort to come to the emergency room? After many sleepless nights and inner turmoil, I decided to do nothing about this incident; he was my friend after all.

Until now, I shudder with disgust from my friend's behavior. I shudder with more disgust from the failure to report my friend's fraudulent action. I sincerely hope that writing about this incident might finally give me the desired catharsis. More importantly, this incident should convince us that, yes, doctors are not immune from greed. And fraud and irresponsible behavior too. The adage, 'do no harm,' addresses the active harming of patients but it doesn't apply to the passive harm that's inflicted on all of us by abuses like this one and many others committed, in the majority of cases, by smart doctors who know how not to harm, but know enough to make their money.

One day, I saw a patient in my office for a second opinion. He was scheduled for ear surgery, but he had doubts about the surgeon in the big city. It happened that I knew that particular surgeon who was famous for doing surgical reconstruction of the hearing mechanism in the ear. Similar to other surgeons, his technique required two or three staged operations on the same ear. To my surprise, that particular doctor had already operated eight times on that particular patient's ear and was planning to operate on it for the ninth time. This poor patient had finally realized the futility of these endless operations, thus he looked for my opinion. If the first operation didn't work, may be the second or the third might, but nine! Equally tragic is that that surgeon usually charges $10,000 for this type of surgery. 10,000 x 8 means that $80,000 were drained from our collective premiums with no benefit to anyone except to that doctor who, I am sure, did the math beforehand. Blessed is the free market and pity the fools who don't have any protection from the law. And the same abuses go on and on.

A friend of mine who works in the U.N. called me at home to ask for my advice. His daughter, who was 10 years old, suffered from frequent ear problems. The consultant in the city performed hearing tests and tympanograms and obtained a scan on her ears. After he treated her with many antibiotics, he diagnosed a cholesteatoma (a condition in which the skin of the drum invaginates into the middle ear and mastoid bone with destructive results), for which he advised a big mastoid operation.

I knew that the incidence of cholesteatoma had become very rare especially after the introduction of myringotomy (putting tubes in the drums) and with the standard and aggressive use of antibiotics. While still on the phone, I asked him to let his daughter blow out her pinched nose to pup the ears, which she did and immediately reported improvement of her hearing. I asked the father to bring his daughter to my office so that I might examine her ears and give him my honest opinion.

My suspicion was correct. She didn't have a cholesteatoma. Her drum was retracted into the middle ear, but I could bring it back to its neutral position by a simple maneuver called pneumatic otoscopy where a negative pressure is created on the outside of the drum. This meant that the retraction was not a cholesteatoma, but the result of negative pressure in the middle ear space sucking the drum inward. It could be easily corrected by inserting a ventilating tube in the drum, or what we call myringotomy.

19

This is exactly what I did. As expected, the drum regained its strength and its normal position, and the hearing returned to its normal level.

I wasn't smarter than the city doctor. Actually, he was a professor in a big city medical center. However, I was absolutely sure that our differing opinions were dictated by different motives.

The original fee-for-service system of compensating doctors and hospitals for their services is based on the simple formula of 80/20 percent where the insurance company pays 80% of any submitted charges, and the patient is responsible for the remaining 20%. Sounds reasonable: the insurance funds wouldn't be depleted by paying 100% of the cost thus keeping the premiums at an affordable level, and the patient would have the incentive to monitor his out-of-pocket expense thus, hopefully, he would become a better consumer of our health care dollars.

I trusted in the claimed benefits of that system until I met a patient who negotiated my surgical fee. She asked me to exaggerate my fee so that her insurance 80% payment would equal my original fee thus she wouldn't have to pay the required 20%. When I refused to do that, she told me that I was naïve not to do it. Other doctors whom she dealt with, she explained, did it as a routine and as a service to their patients!

I confirmed the truth of her statement by hearing it from other doctors. One of them actually got mad at me when I told him about this incident as he figured out that my reduced fees must have brought down the mean of the prevailing and customary levels that the insurance companies used for reimbursement.

Other abuses are inherent in the accepted medical practices we faithfully adhere to. During one of our ENT society's meetings, the discussion turned to reimbursement for fibroptic laryngoscopy (examination of the voice box by a flexible scope introduced through the nose). Only a small number of the doctors present, including myself, didn't charge for this procedure. The majority, however, were getting few hundred dollars for it. I vehemently argued against this practice, emphasizing that our duty was to make a diagnosis with whatever tools we had. We had always been able to see the larynx indirectly with a mirror and we had never charged for its use. Allowing a charge for the use of the flexible scope might invite the greedy to overuse it even if it was not technically necessary.

Needless to say that this abuse didn't only expand, but it also became the 'accepted practice.' All of us are paying for this abusive culture of "standard medical practice."

The fact is that professionals, no matter what profession they practice, are notorious for creating work for themselves. All of us had experiences with the auto mechanic who charged us for extra repairs that we suspected were not necessary or the plumber whom we called to fix one problem and ended up paying for extra repairs we didn't anticipate or thought to be unnecessary.

I was suckered myself by a chimneysweeper when I answered his ad to clean my chimney for the advertised price of $30. After cleaning the chimney, he told me that its top casing was broken and that might represent a hazard to my house. He offered to fix it on the spot for an extra $100. How could I refuse to save my house for this extra $100? After finishing this repair, he came back with another problem. I shouldn't leave the top of my chimney open like it was. He sold me two covers for another $200. I thanked him for his foresight and help, but he had another surprise: the body of the chimney was starting to crack, and he recommended fixing it for another $100. That's when I realized what a fool I was. I refused his last recommendation and reluctantly paid him for the work I had foolishly authorized. The chimney is still standing and nothing bad happened to my house. It was a costly learning experience for me, but a profitable scam for him.

Change the chimneysweeper with doctor or lawyer, or any other professional for that matter, and you have the same result.

In health care, consumers/patients and doctors justify these abuses by the refrain: "it's only insurance money." What an unconscionable and ignorant attitude! All of our health care expenditure comes from our pockets whether paid by the government (taxes), insurance companies (premiums), or indirectly in the form of coinsurance or additional costs that are added to the price of the consumer products we buy to cover the manufacturer's expense for the health care coverage of his employees. This is a fact that has to be made clear. All of us must have a vested interest on how this money is spent.

Other types of greed are commonly justified by the fear of liability and malpractice suits.

I knew of a colleague who performed a hearing test on every patient who had earwax. When I objected to this absurd practice, he defended his actions by invoking the liability issue - one of his patients claimed that her hearing had diminished after he removed wax from her ears, and he wanted to protect himself from possible liability. I asked if he really believed in what he was doing. He answered, "why not. It is another source of income."

Making money can still be easy even if our overhead expenses, like the malpractice insurance, increased.

A large hike in the malpractice premiums was planned in the late seventies. I was talking with one of the surgeons when he told me that he had already increased his fees even before the higher premiums took effect. As he had figured it out, he would even make more money and blame the malpractice crisis as his excuse. The insurance companies that were established after that crisis are making unprecedented profits and are now sitting on such large reserves that some of them are giving huge dividends and acquiring new companies.

Even the fear of cancer doesn't escape exploitation.

I performed a laryngectomy on a patient and we became good friends. He referred all his family to me. Subsequently, I saw one of his brothers for a check up. He was understandably worried about cancer. After a thorough examination, using my eyes and hands only, I didn't find any cancer in his head and neck area, and I reassured him about that.

He disappeared for a couple of years. When he unexpectedly showed up in my office, he started to apologize. He asked for my forgiveness because he was seeing another doctor for the past few years; the other doctor was participating in his insurance plan and I was not. He then told me that he underwent two biopsy procedures on his larynx that didn't show any cancer. He came back to me because the other doctor was "pushing" for a third biopsy, and the patient obviously had doubts about the need for it. That's why he came back to me.

I carefully examined his larynx, and there was no doubt in my mind that his larynx was normal. I advised against the third biopsy, and he was relieved by my reassurance. He then told me that he suspected that the other doctor was exploiting him to make more money. Shortly thereafter, this particular doctor was investigated for fraud. He was found guilty and subsequently lost his license but not before he had accumulated a fortune that enabled him to live happily and lavishly in sunny Florida.

The rampant abuse of modern technology added more venues for us to make more money: it made it easy to sell new services and procedures whether they were necessary or not. We have to remember here that most of our procedures are elective and some are of questionable value even if we sell them for the assumed improvement of the quality of our lives.

Laser surgery stands out in the forefront as an example of the abuse of technology. Patients think of it as the stuff of "Star Wars" and the magic weapon for any procedure they need - they want laser for any operation you recommend to them. And the surgeons use this mystique to promote its use even if there are no proper indications for it. They charge more for its use, and this technology became another source of making more money. The fact remains that, as miraculous as it is for specific eye and endoscopic procedures, it is nothing more than another cutting tool.

The fact remains that the amount of payment allowed by the insurance companies for any procedure actually determines the indications for doing or not doing it.

Athroscopic knee surgery came into existence with the introduction of the arthroscope. A scope is inserted through tiny incisions to examine the inside of the knee and remove torn cartilage. Thousands of these procedures are performed every day all over the country. I am not concerned here about the merits or benefits of this operation, though I have my own doubts. However, I couldn't help but notice the astronomical increase in these numbers once reimbursement for it decreased. Orthopedic surgeons used to charge $3,000-10,000, depending on where you happen to be in the country, for knee arthroscopy. With the new payment of only a few hundred dollars by the insurance companies, more volume became the way to make the difference, and "volume" became the new mantra.

Paradoxically, the reverse happened in the case of tonsillectomy in the ENT practice. The number of tonsillectomies decreased with the decrease in the reimbursement for it. This contradiction, I believe, is due to the difference in how each specialty makes its money. The ENT field can be lucrative with office practice only, even without the extra income from surgery.

We doctors can always justify any trend that brings us money. We can always rely on conflicting articles in reputable medical journals. It all depends on whom you quote - there is always a hidden article somewhere that can justify whatever you chose to do. This is the nature of the inexact science of medicine. Standardizing the care is not the answer because each individual patient has different sets of social, psychological and moral perspective than every other patient even if they have the same diagnosis. Eliminating the greed completely is impossible. The obvious goal in any system that we adopt to manage our health care should be to lessen the possibility of such abuse. This can, and should, be done.

Malpractice

One night, I was taking a middle-aged woman to the operating room to control profuse nose bleeding that continued unabated despite all the conservative measures that we had already tried. Surgery was the only option left to locate and seal the bleeding source. While I was talking to her outside the door to the O.R., she surprised me when she whispered in my ear, "Doctor," she said, "I hope that you make a small mistake, though not a serious one, so I can sue you." She then immediately apologized saying that she was only kidding.

Kidding or not, this incident opened my eyes to a hidden aspect of medical malpractice. This woman wasn't a bad or a malicious person: I had known her for many years, and, I thought that we were good friends. If she could utter those words when her life was literally in my hands, there must have been something sinister hidden in her psyche, and in other patients'

28

psyches, dreaming of winning a painless and lucrative lottery. It is the same greed that makes us sue each other following car accidents, falling on our neighbor's sidewalk or spilling on ourselves hot coffee that we bought in a fast food restaurant. Can't we be sensible enough to see the danger in this explosion of unnecessary and costly litigation? If health care reform is needed, legal reform is a must.

Contrast this incident in the case of the above bleeding patient with my experience in the case of a British teenager who developed a brain abscess after I performed nasal surgery on him to correct a deviated septum. He was a cleft palate patient who had already gone through few reconstructive procedures, and the nasal surgery was the last step in his rehabilitation process. As usually done following this type of surgery, I used nasal packing to support the septum and prevent the bleeding. I also put him on prophylactic antibiotics to fore guard against the possibility of infection that might result from the packing. I removed the nasal packing after one day. When I saw him in my office after one week, he was complaining of persistent headaches and fever. When I moved his neck, I detected neck rigidity, which made me suspect an intracranial complication like meningitis or brain abscess. I immediately admitted him to the hospital, obtained a scan and brought a neurosurgeon to see him. The diagnosis of a brain abscess was confirmed. In less than one hour, the Neurosurgeon drained the brain abscess, and my patient recovered completely without any residual damage His mother told me later on that her American friend advised her to sue me for this unexpected complication that was "inflicted" on her son. However, she refused to act on her neighbor's advice. "Doctor," she told me in her British accent, "this complication is not your fault. I am actually grateful to you for suspecting this abscess and taking immediate action to treat it."

This British woman acted differently than what her American neighbor might have done. Although both came from the same stock and influenced by the same culture, they grew up in two different legal systems. Untoward results from medical care are not confined to America; they do happen equally often and possibly more in other countries but America's cost for medical liability far exceeds that of all other countries combined. The reason is obvious: Our legal system allows, and unfortunately encourages, that to happen. I assume that getting a share out of this huge pot of money invites our lawyers to keep it that way.

My virginity in the world of malpractice unexpectedly ended when one of my patients sued me. She was a girl in her late teens when I first saw her and performed an operation on her nose.

The story began when she came to my office complaining of nasal obstruction and stating a desire to have a nose job. My evaluation showed a deviated septum as the cause of her breathing problem. The structure of her face was strong and impressive that I predicted the potential for a beautiful look if minor changes were made in her nose. I explained my findings and the details of the surgery to her and to her mother who was with her. They wanted the surgery done.

I took the standard four photographs of her face. The first was the frontal view, which showed the nose in relation to the length and width of the face. Her nose was relatively long and its tip was drooping and hiding the full impact of her smile. The second and third views were of the right and left profiles, which showed a hump on the bridge of the nose and brought to a better focus the excessive length of the nose and its droopy tip. The last view was that of the base of the nose, the nostrils, which showed an obvious shift of the lower edge of the septum to one side causing asymmetry of the nostrils and obstructing one of them. I remember telling her jokingly that only lovers and dogs see this view: lovers when they lie on your chest and dogs when they look up at you from the ground.

The surgery went well. I liked what I saw when I removed the dressing one week later. She cried with happiness when she saw her new nose in the mirror. Her mother came in and expressed complete satisfaction with the result. I saw her again after another week when the swelling and bruising had subsided, and I took my first set of post - operative

31

photographs. I was happy. She was ecstatic. We agreed that she would return in another month for follow up.

She came back after one year. In the meantime, the young and timid girl had changed into a fully blossomed and assertive woman. Her new look gave me pride in my work but I was more gratified by the positive change in her personality.

"I am happy to see you," I said.

She looked at me with obvious anger and said, "I am not happy."

I looked at her in surprise, unable to detect the source of her unhappiness. The nose looked well proportioned and exactly right for her face. She was not only beautiful, but stunningly so.

"Your nose looks really beautiful. You just have to tell me what makes you unhappy," I said.

She turned her head backwards and pointed to her nostrils saying, "You see this lower edge of the septum? It is curving again, and I don't like it."

I noticed a slight shift of the septum, which was not obvious unless you looked carefully from below.

I was aware of the fixation phenomenon in patients who undergo cosmetic surgery. They become more critical and often see insignificant asymmetries they never had noticed before. With this awareness in mind, I didn't dismiss her worries nor did I ignore them.

"You're right. But you really have to look hard to see it," I said.

She interrupted me with an obvious angry and aggressive voice. "I see it and I don't like it."

I showed her the previous photographs pointing to the obvious improvement. She looked only casually at the photographs and appeared resigned on a definite goal in her mind.

When I offered a second operation to correct this problem, she promised to think it over and to let me know.

The next time I heard from her was through a summons from her lawyer. She was suing me for negligence. She and her lawyer were asking for twenty million dollars!

Everybody told me not to worry: this was part of doing business and my insurance company would take care of me. But nobody would understand the horrendous and devastating impact of receiving a summons as a doctor who had received one. It feels like a violation of the essence of your professional competence and a serious threat to your career and livelihood. No logic can explain this feeling.

I reported this summons to my insurance company, and indeed they said that they would take care of it. However, they advised me to retain another lawyer at my own expense because the plaintiff was asking for much more than the limits of my insurance coverage. I had never been frightened as much in my life. I immediately consulted a lawyer friend of mine who reassured me that the twenty million dollar amount was a tactic used by lawyers to produce exactly the same intended effect as had happened with me. They were aiming for a settlement.

You have to be personally involved in a lawsuit to appreciate the tragic state of our legal system. It is like a sword on the front of your neck that makes an initial superficial cut in your skin that burns and hurts. Then the sword disappears and the wound heals. With the passing of time, you forget the whole problem, consciously or subconsciously. Then, after a few months have passed by, the sword suddenly comes back in the form of an unexpected call from your lawyer. And the wound opens again. Sleepless nights follow, but mercifully, the healing power of the good old time brings you back to your normal sanity. No more news for a few more months and you think that you're safe. Well, think again. Lawyers must have been taught how to bleed you without killing you. They schedule what they call "examination before trial" (EBT) where the plaintiff's lawyer asks you questions and you answer them. Fine, you say - you're ready. You cancel your surgeries and your office appointments on that day.

Not so fast! They cancel the hearing on a short notice and they give you another date to be cancelled, rescheduled, and cancelled again and again. And the wound festers and gets deeper until the EBT actually occurs.

Your lawyer wants to meet with you before the EBT to brief you and to instruct you on how to talk, dress and behave. "Dress in a dark suit. Don't answer any questions I object to. Don't volunteer any information..." He makes you think that you are a criminal and that you have already lost your case.

When my EBT actually happened, I went to my lawyer's office, where the meeting was supposed to take place, a few minutes early. The plaintiff's lawyer arrived shortly thereafter accompanied by my patient, - my once satisfied patient now turned enemy. My lawyer took me aside to tell me that she was beautiful. I smiled and told him that I am the one who made her beautiful. Seeing the result of my work gave me much needed confidence and reassurance.

Over the next few hours I was asked by the plaintiff's lawyer about my name, address, educational history, training, hospital appointments, society memberships, publications and many other details that had nothing do with the problem at hand. In addition, all that information was already available through my CV that was handed to him before the meeting.

"Don't mind me, doctor," he repeatedly said. "This is only for the record." This "for the record" interrogation took up the whole morning session.

We resumed the hearing after a lunch break. The plaintiff's lawyer asked me about anatomical details of the nose that he appeared not be interested in or to understand their relevance to his case. Subsequently, he made me read, for the record, and explain every word I wrote in my office and hospital charts. Both charts were small, and the information they revealed was accurate and self-explanatory that it shouldn't take more than a few minutes to go through them. Still, it took us few more hours to finish with this exercise. He had a genius for twisting words and for repeating the same questions in different ways and with different tones. The photographs came last. He had nothing to say about them. Every peace of paper was marked as an exhibit that I was supposed to safely keep until the "trial." Yes, THE TRIAL.

A full day and a lot of money were wasted, I believe, intentionally in an exercise in futility. They tell me, that's how the system works. I say, from personal experience, that the system has been corrupted and it should be reformed.

But let's go back to my attractive 'enemy.' I felt better after seeing the beautiful and durable result I accomplished for her. The EBT also went well as my lawyer had told me. Subsequently, my painful wound started to heal. When my insurance company asked my permission to settle the case out of court, I refused. They thought that they could settle this case for $25,000, which was much less than what it would cost them to go to court. (The plaintiff's lawyer knew that too.) My lawyer didn't force me to settle, he left that decision up to me. I was heading for a court hearing even if they called it 'a trial.'

Nothing happened for another year. Seeing the enemy in person had dulled the sword that was against my neck. However, they knew how to injure you even with a dull sword.

My case was coming up in the next court session. When they gave me a date, it wasn't a final date. I was supposed to make myself available on a short notice, and we went back to the waiting game. I had to cancel my surgeries and my office appointments time and again until I lost confidence in their schedule.

In the mean time, my family planned a trip to Mexico. However, a few days before our departure, my lawyer called with the final date for the court hearing, which would have fallen during my vacation.

I offered to cancel my trip and make myself available for the court hearing. He surprised me by insisting that I go ahead with my travel plans. He promised that he would postpone the hearing, and if he failed, he would

Fouad B. Michael, M.D.

call me to return if that became necessary. I gave him the name of the hotel where I would be staying, and I left for Mexico.

He was true to his promise: he called me in Mexico. He also had a great surprise: The suit was withdrawn. And I became a free man.

When I was hit by another malpractice suit, I couldn't see myself going through the same ordeal; I quickly gave my consent for my insurance company to settle.

The tragic fact about medical malpractice is that the injured patient gets only part of the settlement after the lawyers get their contingency fee, which amounts to 30% - 50% of the total award, plus the expense they incur, which is known to be inflated as a routine by all lawyers. They bill by the hour. Even telephone calls can add up to many hours.

(This reminds me of the joke about a lawyer who died at the age of 35. When he met God, he objected to his untimely death. "God, you have made a mistake. I am only 35, and I shouldn't have died at this young age," he told God. God looked at him in surprise and reassured him that he would go and check his records. When God came back, he said to the lawyer, "Son, we didn't make a mistake. Our records show that your age is 75, not 35 as you claim. You see, by the hours you billed, we figured out that you are actually 75 years old.")

Remember the class action suit against Corning for the supposedly disease -inducing breast implants? My concern here is not the validity of the claim, but I wonder how many members of the public realized that one law firm was getting hundreds of millions of dollars, while each patient who was involved in this class action suit was getting only a few thousand. Think about it! The same scenario happened with the tobacco settlement: lawyers collected over 40 billion dollars. Yes, 40 billion! This much money would have bought treatment for all the patients who suffered from the harmful effects of tobacco with enough money left over for a campaign to combat smoking. More recently a class action suit was filed against a car company for injuries to owners of a specific defective car model. In a settlement, lawyers collected twenty five million dollars while the injured motorists received coupons for five hundred dollars redeemable when they buy another car.

The added expense from medical litigation costs us tens of billions of dollars that are removed from patient care. It is estimated that malpractice premiums add at least ten billion dollars to the doctors' overhead and another 100 billion dollars in defensive medicine. More tragic is the fact that the malpractice threat doesn't decrease the number of bad outcomes and that the majority of injured patients do not file malpractice suits - most of the time they accept less than adequate care, and some time, negligent care due to the fact that doctoring gives doctors great power and legitimacy. It is also a fact that bad doctors are sued less often than the good ones who are doing the most complicated and the more risky procedures that potentially result in the majority of the malpractice cases.

I knew of a surgeon who severed the esophagus during removal of the voice box for cancer. It shouldn't have had happened if he knew what he was doing. A stricture or narrowing of the esophagus resulted. The patient suffered from difficulty in swallowing for the rest of his life but the doctor was never sued. God knows how many incompetent doctors have committed mistakes but they were never sued for malpractice.

I knew of another doctor who did the wrong operation on a patient. His patient had difficulty swallowing. She had an obvious goiter that the doctor ignored, and performed on her Cricothyrotomy. (This entails dividing the sphincter muscle in the upper esophagus.) And he made money performing this operation. When her swallowing problem didn't improve, he went back and did the right operation by removing her thyroid gland. He, too, was never sued.

On the other hand, what we call defensive medicine doesn't only cost us too much money it can also cost us a lot of pain and suffering when the fear of liability drives away some doctors from pursuing risky but effective treatment or surgery.

I was operating on a patient for cancer of the voice box. I scheduled him for total laryngectomy and removal of the nodes of his neck. (Radical Neck Dissection) The patient was in good general condition, and his internist cleared him for the planned surgery.

During the middle of the neck dissection, the anesthesiologist asked me to abort the operation. He claimed that the patient's blood pressure was too low to safely carry him through this extended operation. I asked the anesthesiologist to use fluids or blood or even some medications that would elevate the blood pressure, any of which he was supposed to do anyway, but he refused. He insisted that he wouldn't assume the responsibility if anything bad happened. I appealed to his chief, but he too invoked the risk of liability. They gave me no choice but to stop the surgery and close the incisions. This happened when I was still considered as a foreigner and undesirable.

The patient's internist saw him again that same day. He agreed that the surgery shouldn't have been cancelled, and he cleared him for the surgery again.

I knew that opening the neck and cutting around the cancer without removing it would risk its spread and expose the patient to a poorer prognosis. I tried to reschedule the surgery for the next day, but there was no way that I could get the needed 6-8 hours of operating room time that quickly, a privilege reserved for the well connected and preferred surgeons - at the time, I was also new on the hospital staff without the needed clout in the established hospital hierarchy. A few more valuable days elapsed before I could finish that operation.

As expected, the cancer started to appear around the incisions in a few weeks. The patient ultimately died, but not before unnecessary suffering. There was no doubt in my mind that the fear of liability and defensive medicine had cost this patient his life. This is certainly a different side effect from the malpractice problem than the usually quoted one of cost and the unnecessary tests. Doctors sometimes actually shy from giving the proper care if they think that it will expose them to malpractice suits.

As surgical complications generate the majority of malpractice suits and complications are bound to happen if you do enough surgeries, I like to quote a famous saying in the surgical field: "The surgeon who does not have complications is the surgeon who does not operate." In one of the ENT meetings I attended, the discussion turned to post–operative bleeding, its causes and the ways to prevent it. After a lengthy discussion on the required tests and the surgical techniques, one of the more experienced surgeons said, "You forgot to mention that they (the patients) bleed because we cut them." How true.

If we can muster the guts to face the trial lawyers' powerful lobby and change our tort system, we can improve, if not completely abolish, most of the side effects of liability in health care. I suggest the following reforms.

1-   Replace jury trials with an arbitration system where a panel of doctors, lawyers and laypersons headed by a judge review and decide on all malpractice cases. This would eliminate the unpredictability of lengthy and expensive trials, the injured patient would be compensated quickly, and the guilty doctor would be dealt with appropriately. I know that a trial by jury is a constitutional requirement. However, a jury of peers is also a constitutional requirement. The claim that if this applies to doctors then it should apply to all other professions, which is true if other professions are as complicated as medicine. Doctors go through a lengthy education and long years of training. In addition, medical practice is much more complicated to be properly understood by a layperson, which is hardly the case in other professions. Even if arbitration is not politically feasible, why don't we mandate that the losing party in a jury trial pay the cost of the litigation? This is the standard practice in all other civilized countries. Lawyers would then be more careful not to initiate frivolous suits, and they would have to work hard to establish the merits of their cases beforehand.

2-   Forbid settlements. People, with encouragement from their lawyers, file suits right and left. Trial lawyers advertise in the newspapers, radio and TV. In essence they promise, "No fees and no worries. Just come to us and we'll make you rich!" Lucrative settlements are behind this frenzy. They know that in the majority of cases, litigation would lead to payment by settlement because it is more costly for defendants and their insurance companies to pursue the ordeal of a court hearing than to settle. We should also be concerned with the fact that medical malpractice settlements imply no assumption of guilt or responsibility on the part of the doctors involved. We need verdicts, and we should have the right to know for sure who is negligent and who is not.

3-   Put a limit on pain and suffering awards. Actuarial tables are used to calculate loss of income due to injury or death. However, there is no way that we can put a value on pain and suffering. Lawyers and patients use this loophole to enrich themselves. We should compensate the injured, but we should be sensible enough to put a limit on this elusive subject of pain and suffering. The same is true of punitive awards. In both cases, at least half of the money goes to the lawyers. This only makes the lawyers richer but it leaves the injured patient with much less money and leaves the potentially negligent doctor to continue in his practice.

4-   Punish the doctors who commit flagrant malpractice, but protect the ones who commit errors of judgment. The bad apples should be eliminated by recommendation from the arbitration panel. This recommendation should then be sent and acted upon by the states' professional misconduct boards.

5-   Eliminate the contingency fees. Lawyers have no inherent right to collect 30% - 50% of malpractice rewards. The injured patients should be the sole beneficiaries. Lawyers would then be discouraged from filing frivolous suits, and they would have to work for their pay like everybody else.

Legal reform is a prerequisite for any meaningful health care reform. We just have to do it.

Advertising and Consumerism

These two words are so closely interconnected that it is very hard to talk about one without touching on the other as the following stories illustrate.

One day, a young man asked my help for "chronic sinus headaches". My examination showed a deviated nasal septum but no evidence of sinus infection. He did not believe me, mentioning that few other doctors had treated his 'sinus problem' as sinus infection with antibiotics, decongestants, antihistamines, and nasal steroids. They couldn't be all wrong. He insisted on getting a CT scan. I had no choice but to order this study.

As I had expected, the CT scan showed normal sinuses. He still wanted antibiotics, because they had helped him before. This time, I stood my grounds and refused to give him the antibiotics he wanted. Instead, I recommended surgery to correct his deviated septum.

It took him a few months to make up his mind. When he returned, he wanted the surgery done by laser. As much as I tried to explain that laser had no place in this operation, he refused to understand that, and he insisted on the laser. "His friend had his operation done with the laser and he saw advertisements about it," he said. Thankfully for me, I lost "his business".

Countless other patients presented to me with "sinus headaches". After my evaluation, the majority of them turned out to be suffering from migraines or tension headaches. Without exception, all of them had already received many antibiotics, decongestants, and antihistamines without help. Some of these patients accepted my judgment. The vast majority, however, didn't. They still wanted the antibiotics, the antihistamines and the CT scans. That's what advertising and the famous refrain "ask your doctor" had conditioned them to become, consumers.

The overuse of diagnostic technologies is rampant. It is not only that doctors overuse them but also patients demand them like what happened in the following stories.

An old woman came to my office because of dizziness. She had already seen a neurologist who did reassure her about the absence of any serious pathology. He referred her to me to see if her dizziness was due to an inner ear problem. My evaluation did not reveal any ear problem, and

I advised her of that. In addition to the reassurance, I instructed her to perform "Vestibular Exercises" to improve her balance on the assumption that she had Benign Positional Vertigo. (As its name implies, this is a benign problem that can be helped by certain exercises.) This wasn't good enough for her. She wanted an MRI. A friend of hers had a similar problem and her doctor got an MRI for her, she said. I tried as hard as I could to explain that the MRI was not a treatment and that I was sure that she would get better on the exercises, but she refused to listen to me. Suffice it to say that I lost another "customer".

A middle-age woman came to my office one day complaining of hoarseness of voice. I knew that she was a nun, because "sister" was written before her name on the chart - nuns don't have to adhere to a dress code anymore. She didn't smoke, and she seemed to be very cooperative that I was able to see her larynx easily with the mirror (this is done by pushing a warm mirror against the soft palate, which gives you a mirror image of the voice box). That's what I did, and I found that her larynx was normal. I informed her of that. And, I took her through the proper way of projecting her voice and performing deep breathing exercises. End of the story, but it turned out to be otherwise.

That same afternoon, my secretary called me at home with a very disturbing message. This patient called to tell me that I had insulted her intelligence by not doing a fiber-optic examination of her larynx (this is done by inserting a fiber-optic cord through the nose and threading it down the throat to see the voice box directly). "She threatened to report me to all the medical authorities," my secretary informed me with apparent apprehension and advised me to call this patient back.

I immediately called her back. A torrent of insults and threats came out of the telephone that I didn't have a chance to explain anything. How could I have had done that to her, she said, when she was an educated woman with a master degree and a responsible administrative job. She knew, she went on, that I should have had examined her larynx with the fiber-optic laryngoscope, which I didn't. Her voice was intense with anger and the flow of her words was persistent and not amenable to interruption. Ultimately, and with great difficulty, I managed to let her listen. I told her that my duty was to see her larynx and make the right diagnosis of her problem, which I did. Thankfully, it was easy to see her larynx with the mirror, I explained, which made the laryngoscopic examination unnecessary. I also explained that I have saved her a procedure and her insurance company an expense that might have had amounted to a few hundred dollars. She didn't accept my explanation. At the end, similar to what she said to my secretary, she threatened to report me to the hospital administration and to the medical society.

She must have discovered the truth of what I had told her; I didn't hear from the hospital or from the medical society.

This is not meant to be a judgment on these patients, but stories like these certainly point to fundamental issues in health care: Incessant news media coverage that misrepresented medical news, unconscionable advertising campaigns from pharmaceutical companies, doctors, hospitals and suppliers, and irresponsible doctors who catered to profit motives and business demands rather than the well being of patients and the real cost of health care.

Diagnostic tests are not an end by themselves; they are only helpful in making intelligent diagnosis, period. I always said to my students that if you can feel it, see it, or know it, there should be no need for diagnostic tests. However, if tests are needed, get only the necessary ones but not the usual 'battery' of tests. To blindly test every patient speaks only of ignorance and can be done anyway by any moron who has no medical knowledge or training.

I suggest that we conduct a national study to collect data from one of these diagnostic studies, say CT scans, and find out how many were done in one 12 month period, how many were positive, and how many of them changed the patient's management and outcome. I do not have to wait for this study. I am certain that there is sizable overuse and abuse of these diagnostic studies.

The introduction of Functional Endoscopic Sinus Surgery (FESS) in the Ear, Nose, and Throat practice revolutionized the way we treat sinus problems. At the same time it ushered in the explosive use of endoscopic examinations and CT scans. Every sinus complaint now, deservedly or not, warrants endoscopic examination and scanning. Patients expect that, and doctors encourage it. Nasal endoscopy and scanning became the pipeline to produce more customers for this lucrative operation. Doctors get paid for the endoscopic examination. They get paid for the scanning. And they get paid even more for doing the surgery. And FESS became a boom for our specialty.

Thousands of FESSs are performed every year. Well and good if this improves our health. I have my own doubts. Besides, this operation carries the potential for serious complications. I know of many incidents of CSF (the fluid around the brain) leaks, (I had one of my own,) severe and sometimes fatal hemorrhage and even blindness resulting from Endoscopic Sinus Surgery. This doesn't deter us from doing more and more of it.

A new Otolaryngologist joined the staff of our hospital. During my initial conversation with him, we talked about Endoscopic Sinus Surgery. I made it clear that he should be careful and accurate about his indications and to do only the absolutely necessary surgeries. However, I knew later on that he was doing a large number of this operation. After a couple of years, this subject came up again. He honestly admitted that most of his patients did not get much help. He still continued to do more FESS's even after he encountered complications from doing them.

An astonishing surprise came my way from an article in a medical journal in which the author was reporting on the beneficial outcome from this operation on patients with headaches and with NORMAL scans of their sinuses! After operating on hundreds of these patients, he recommended this operation for headaches. I couldn't believe my eyes. My letter to the editor was not published. However they published a milder one criticizing this article.

Millions of patients complain of 'sinus headaches,' stuffy noses, facial pains and postnasal drip. Some of them would have abnormal Ct Scans despite normal clinical findings and others would have the reverse of that. When to operate becomes then a matter of judgment and the door becomes wide open for abuse. The following story illustrates this point.

A young woman with chronic 'sinus' history had a CT scan that showed cloudy sinuses. When I examined her I didn't see any evidence of obstruction to her sinuses and I suspected that her problem might be helped by medical, but not surgical, treatment. I didn't see her again, but I knew her subsequent story as the word spreads around in our small community.

Another surgeon operated on her sinuses on the basis of the abnormal CT scan. It seems that her problem remained the same. Another CT scan showed the same previous pathology. Because her symptoms were localized to one side, our surgeon recommended surgery on that side only. During the second operation, he looked in one side, and apparently was not impressed by his findings. He proceeded to operate on the other side.

In the recovery room, he accidentally looked at the consent form and realized that he had operated on the wrong side. After informing her family, he took the patient back and operated on the correct side she had consented to.

Consumerism, whether practiced by patients or abused by some greedy doctors, has its origin in many sources. I am especially concerned here with one source, and I believe it to be one of the worst disasters that ever happened in our health care system. By this I mean advertising.

Advertising is meant to publicize and bring to the attention of the consumer specific services or products. The motive here is not altruistic. The obvious reason is to present these services and products in a favorable way and to encourage the consumer to consume them. Fair enough. But let's see what happens in the real world.

Douglas Martin of the New York Times wrote an article in the Week in Review on Jan. 9, 2000 titled "What's in a Name: The Allure of Labels" with the theme of power branding in advertisement. Unwittingly, he opened our eyes to the danger of conditioned reflexes when he ended his article by a quote from Dr. Alan Manevitz, a psychiatrist at the New York Presbyterian Hospital: "If you can get a kid at an early age, you can imprint a brand on him". This is the real power, and danger, of advertisement. And this danger came to the field of health care in the late seventies.

Where the well being of the patient is the primary concern of doctors as professionals, the profit and the bottom-line are the driving forces of business. Unfortunately, advertising transformed the medical profession into a business.

Originally, doctors, hospitals, and pharmaceutical companies were not allowed to advertise directly to patients. It was not only unethical to advertise when I started my practice in the early seventies, but also unacceptable to even use over-sized or pretentious shingles. I was told by my seniors to only do a good job and not to worry about soliciting patients. They assured me that the word-of-mouth, satisfied patients and the confidence of my colleagues would guarantee me a good living. All this changed once advertising was allowed and the genie came out of the bottle.

A young woman came to my office with severe nasal problems following a nose job done 3 months earlier. I saw the telltale signs of a mediocre nose job, but my greatest surprise was finding a rotten packing left deep inside her nose. When I removed it and showed it to her, she started to cry. She said that her surgeon dismissed her complaints and told her that he could do nothing more for her. When I asked why she went to that particular surgeon, she told me that she listened to his advertisement.

This is not an anecdotal story. I can tell you of many other countless patients who use doctor's services solely on the basis of advertisement. And often times, they pay a dear price for that.

Hospital advertising is even worse. We are bombarded by sound bites, sadly enough, from the most prestigious hospitals in the country. Most of us heard the commercials: "take good care of yourself…" "Our doctors see more patients in a month than other doctors' see in a life time…" "If it is for the best medical care you need, there is no difference between traveling a mile or a hundred miles…" "We do minimally invasive surgery…" "We have the best laser surgery." etc, etc.

I am not saying that these big centers are not big or better. However, many other hospitals are as good where the same procedures are done equally well, but they do not have the resources or the clout to join in this advertising frenzy.

A patient of mine chose to go to the big center in the city to have the radical surgery done instead of letting me do it. I am sure that his decision was influenced by the fame of that institution, which is the result of, you guessed it, advertising. A few months later, he came to see me because of difficulty with his speech. I discovered paralysis of one side of his tongue, which I knew it to be the result of injury to the motor nerve that is responsible for the tongue movement, but the patient wasn't told of that injury which happened in the hospital that its advertisement says '… our doctors perform more surgery in a year than other doctors perform in a life time.'

Although these centers are exceptionally prepared and experienced to handle rare and innovative procedures, they have no additional value when it comes to established and routine procedures. In these situations, they have the added disadvantage of poor follow up and impersonal care in addition to their inflated and expensive services. They get the glory, and the income, by doing the procedure, but they usually leave the difficult task of follow up and dealing with the complications, when they happen, to the local doctors - it is not easy for patients to travel long distances if complications or emergencies arise.

Like many other suburban doctors, I had my share of problems to deal with following some surgeries performed in the big city: a life threatening post-op bleeding, a non-healing or infected wound or terminally ill patients after failure of surgery. "Go to your local doctor," that's what they tell them.

The explosion of hospital advertising did not only cross-state lines, but also extended beyond our borders. I frequently receive calls from friends in Egypt enquiring about specific doctors they heard about and were supposed to come and see in the big city. I have no objection to this practice, but when it comes to honesty and ethics, I have to question the motives of soliciting patients from around the world.

A friend and famous writer from Egypt called me to enquire about a surgeon in one of those big centers. My friend's wife had colon cancer that was removed in England. Her cancer recurred one year later and the British doctors determined that it was non-resectable and incurable. They advised against any further treatment.

My friend happened to hear about this surgeon in the big center of the big city. The famous doctor had a telephone conference with them after all the data was faxed and available to him. Yes he could help, and yes they should come.

I called this doctor. The hospital operator referred me to the 'international' department, and I was surprised by the scope and the extent of this part of their business. In any event, the surgeon assured me of his experience and credentials and his ability to help my friend's wife.

The patient came, was transferred directly from the airport to the hospital and in a few days had her surgery done. When I visited her a few days after the operation, I immediately realized that the surgery was a failure. From the facts I had, including the opinion of the British doctors, I knew that this famous doctor had done an unnecessary surgery. He made his money, and my friend's wife died shortly thereafter.

The damage done by advertising from doctors and hospitals is nothing compared to that of the pharmaceutical companies. (More on that in the next chapter.) All of us have seen TV commercials promoting drugs, some with scary tactics, and others with false promise of cures, and doctors get these "consumers" demanding these drugs. Even over-the-counter (OTC) medications are pushed on the poor consumer with the resulting waste of billions of health care dollars. With these OTC medications, no proof of effectiveness or worth is required, and no regulatory mechanism is in place.

Guess who pays for all this fortune that's poured into the advertising coffers? That's all of us. This money is criminally stolen from our health care and unconscionably shifted to line the pockets of Madison Avenue executives, pharmaceutical companies, doctors, and hospitals. Advertising in health care should be banned. Period.

The Pharmaceutical Industry

When a U. S. Representative takes elderly constituents to Canada to buy prescription drugs at lower prices than in the U. S., this speaks a lot about our pharmaceutical industry. This is what Representative Bernard Saunders of Vermont actually did.

When the Maine Legislature approves a bill to mandate that all drugs sold in the state cost no more than they would in Canada, and when we know that our cost is 60 to 80 percent higher, we have to wonder.

What is happening to us? How did it come to this level where every greedy entity is dipping into the huge pot of our health care dollars?

Pharmaceutical companies claim that the high price they charge for drugs is justified by the high expense they incur in research and development, R & D. This is a false and deceptive claim. R & D is not the whole story. They want us to ignore that their stocks are traded in the stock market where shareholders and traders are making unprecedented profits for reasons unrelated to our health. They want us to ignore the astronomical figures they give to their CEOs and waste on administrative cost. Above all, they want us to ignore the billions of dollars they spend on advertising. They actually spend 18 billion dollars, (50 billion if you include direct patient advertising to this figure,) on advertising compared to 8 billion on research. I am not a mathematician, but you don't have to be one to understand the implication from and the significance of these figures. All of that money is much, much more than the cost of their claimed R & D. Moreover, how come, then, that the drugs that are developed by foreign subsidiaries are still selling at a higher price in the U. S. than in Europe and Canada? Why is it that we in the U. S. have to pay the lion's share of the R & D cost? How come that when some of these new drugs are developed in university labs with government grants, they are still patented by these drug companies for their own enrichment? How come that most drugs have two prices: a costly one for the uninsured and a cheaper one for the insured?

A recent report from the Department of Health and Human Services showed that Medicare beneficiaries who lack drug coverage are charged significantly more than the ones who have drug coverage. As Americans are not protected from over-pricing of drugs like other peoples, they are charged more for the same drugs. Similarly, the uninsured have no entity to defend or bargain for them, so they are charged more than the insured patients who have the power of insurance negotiators behind them. The motive behind these abusive practices is profit, not the interest of the patient or the claimed cost for R & D.

Another observation worth mentioning is the fact that whenever a patent for a drug is about to expire, the same company releases a newly patented drug with essentially the same indications. This practice makes me believe that research for new drugs is not totally dictated by the potential benefit to the patients, but mostly by the unconscionable greed of the drug companies. (The expiration of the patent makes the drug available to other competitors and to its generic and cheaper variants.)

Incidentally, cholesterol has become the talisman for the drug companies; Cholesterol-lowering drugs have made huge profits for them. Remember that these drugs are recommended for the life of the patient. (Remember too that blood pressure lowering drugs, which are already out of the patent protection, are also recommended for the lives of the patients, but you certainly see a flood of advertising for the first group of drugs but none for the latter. The sad answer lies in the fact of how much money could be made from each.) In addition to the original statin drugs for lowering cholesterol there came another group of drugs that added more expense to the patients and more profits to the drug companies. I happened to know from personal experience that Niacin, from the vitamin B group, might be as effective as all of the "recommended" expensive drugs.. (Europeans have used Niacin for the treatment of dizziness and as a blood vessel dilator and accidentally came across these assumed benefits. I learned from them to use it for dizziness.) I do not have any scientific evidence to support this claim, however, I know from my Internist, who is a university professor, that Niacin has been known for its cholesterol lowering property for a long time. Therefore, I was happily surprised when a recent recommendation has brought Niacin to the forefront of the fight against cholesterol. It is very cheap and abundantly available over the counter. I hesitate to be cynical, but I have reasonable doubts that the pharmaceutical industry did not elect to reveal this fact sooner than our not-for-profit scientists did.

JAMA (The Journal of the American Medical Association) published a paper in the first week of 2010 evaluating the indications and effectiveness of antidepressants, like Prozac and Paxil. In essence, the researchers found that the pharmaceutical companies had originally tested these drugs on severely depressed patients and reported good results thus secured an approval from the FDA (Food and Drug Administration.) However, according to this paper, 50% of patients diagnosed with depression, and are currently on these drugs, have mild-to-moderate forms and are not helped by antidepressants. These patients did as well on the placebo. Still, these drugs are prescribed indiscriminately and in larger and larger numbers. The pharmaceutical advertising has added more to this overuse by creating more depressed consumers out of normal people, doctors and patients alike. I suspect that the same goes in the case of insomnia. In essence, advertising conditioned the patients not to look for a cause to their sleeplessness, or depression. Just take our pills and you will be happy and sleep like a butterfly!!

Like every other doctor, I had my own experience with pharmaceutical sales persons (they are called reps) who give us many incentives to use particular medications instead of competing ones. It reached a level that they conditioned us to prescribe specific brands from the same group of medications, even if there were no bioactive differences between them. Yes, competition is legal and even desirable. But strangely enough, the competition in the drug industry didn't lower the price for the consumer as if all the pharmaceutical companies have conspired between themselves to keep the price of our medication consistently high; the price differences between two similarly active brands are too miniscule to put a dent on our choice.

When I argued with the reps about the inflated cost of their products, which put a hardship on my patients, they invariably told me to do them a favor and at least prescribe these medications to the patients who had prescription coverage as if the insurance money is not our collective money after all.

How about the majority of our elderly patients who take 10 – 20 pills a day and some pills can cost over $10 each? Many a time, I received calls from patients after they went to the pharmacy with my prescriptions saying that they could not afford to fill them. This is happening in the richest country in the world!

Incentives to prescribe whatever the drug companies want us to prescribe reached a scandalous proportion that the AMA realized the inherent danger of this practice. This forced them to formulate guidelines for what is acceptable and what is not. Personal gifts, free vacations, and payments are out, but donations to medical societies and sponsoring their activities are still ethical.

Ethical or not, the pharmaceutical companies are using every weapon in their arsenal to influence the prescribing habits of doctors and the power of advertising and the news media outlets to generate more and more consumers. If you have any further doubt about this conditioning, just remember the famous refrain: "Ask your doctor."

Back to the drug reps. One time, I pressured one of them to admit that there was no difference between his company's product and a competing one. He conceded that much, but he pointed out that his product was packaged in a non-breakable container! What a moronic reason to choose between competing drugs.

Even when I told the reps that I rarely write prescriptions, they still kept on coming back with more pressure to prescribe their products. I discovered, to my surprise, that drug companies had a profile on my prescribing habits when one rep showed disappointment because I prescribed a competitor's drug more often than his in a specific month. When I asked how he could have possibly known about that, he admitted to the fact that the pharmaceutical companies keep a database on the prescribing habits of each doctor. Strangely enough managed care companies keep the same database on doctors in their panels in an attempt to influence their prescribing habits, in this case, for cheaper drugs. This is how the private for-profit business understands how to make more money by selling more expensive drugs in the case of the pharmaceutical companies, and by encouraging the use of cheaper drugs in the case of the insurance companies. In both cases, profit is the driving force for this behavior, not the wellbeing of patients. And, the sanctity of privacy is thus intentionally violated in both cases.

Well-publicized studies demonstrated errors of prescribing and dispensing drugs. Hundreds of thousands of patients suffer harm and even death each year from these errors. I suggest that we not only develop a more foolproof system to avoid errors, but also a more conscientious culture of prescribing what is absolutely needed for each patient and not succumb to the drug companies' push for more unnecessary use of drugs.

The same abuse can be seen from the pricing of medical supplies.

A representative of one of the medical supplies companies wanted to sell me a headlamp. It is somewhat similar to what the miners use: a head band to which is attached a light source. I had always used the old fashion head mirror worn by the old fashion doctors you see in the cartoons, and I thought that I should catch up with the modern times. The price tag of seven hundred dollars for this modern gadget made me decide otherwise. I kept on using my old head mirror.

The same overpricing is rampant in the case of any product that is needed for medical use. A scissors that sells for a few dollars in the mall is sold for hundreds of dollars to doctors and hospitals. Home care appliances fall in the same abused category. Myriad of companies saw the opportunity for easy profit and dipped into the pot. They advertise in the newspapers, TV and radio, "Just get our products and you don't even have to fill the forms; we'll fill them for you. Medicare and Medicaid will pay for them."

Sadly enough, once you mention medical use, the product is packaged differently and sold for a premium price.

When the government spends $700 for a toilette seat, we raise hell. But when private companies charge $700 for a headband and a bulb, (and by the way, private companies are the ones that charged the government for this $700 toilette seat,) we sing the praises for the free market. Abuse is still abuse, whether practiced by government or private contractors and enterprises.

We shouldn't spare any wealth to care for our sick, but we should deny this wealth to the abusive pharmaceutical and medical supply industries.

Profiteering Parasites

The following story was published in one of the daily newspapers when the FBI was called to investigate a medical, or more correctly business, outfit for apparent and flagrant fraud. The trigger was a $5400 bill for a one-day service for one patient.

The mill was a Chiropractic Rehabilitation Center that treated patients with injuries from work-related and automobile accidents. This outfit owned X ray and scanning facilities and every conceivable testing equipment form electromyography (EMG) that tested the strength of muscles, to nerve conduction probes that tested the function of nerves, to many other machines that could be used in medical care as tools for generating income. Facilities like this one establish their own networks of agents in workplaces and police precincts. They even have their own Gypsy drivers who patrol the streets for possible accidents. An agent refers the injured victim to the facility. The facility pays him for the referral. Another agent in the insurance company gets paid to facilitate the approval of the submitted bills. Hired radiologists get paid to give a favorable reading of X-rays and MRIs. Staff doctors are paid to certify for the necessity of the rehab program for their patients.

The $5400 bill is not unusual. Any back pain complaint triggers a chain of X-rays and MRI tests of every part of the spine, from the cervical and thoracic, to the lower lumber regardless of the location of the pain. And every test of every part is charged separately. EMG is a must as well as nerve conduction testing. A sonogram might even be used. And all this testing that is done in one visit can easily add up to the $5400 bill.

When these bills keep on coming, someone in the insurance company is bound to question them. This was what happened in the case of this particular rehab center. The inflated bill was discovered by a diligent clerk, which triggered the FBI investigation and the fraud charge.

I became personally aware of a similar fraudulent practice when a relative of mine was involved in a car accident in front of his home. A truck suddenly appeared from nowhere at the scene of the accident. Its driver volunteered to take my injured relative to one of those centers. When my relative asked to be taken to the nearest hospital Emergency Room, the driver refused to take him there favoring the outpatient facility. When this was refused, the driver offered him $2000 if he agreed to be taken to that particular facility.

In another incident, a patient of mine who makes a living driving a limousine was involved in a head-on collision. He sustained broken bones, and his car was totaled. The next day, he received a call from a lawyer he never met before offering to represent him to regain the value of his car and collect compensation for his injuries.

During the free consultation, the lawyer wanted him to get his medical care through a specific doctor and pursue a rehab program at another outfit that he recommended. When my relative told the lawyer that his care would be arranged through an orthopedic doctor he knew, the lawyer offered him $5000 if he was retained. He promised a favorable medical report and an extended care that would guarantee a bigger reward. "It doesn't cost you a thing. This is a sure-win case and if you listen to me, you will be rich enough to retire."

My patient hired another lawyer, replaced his car and never retired.

I visited one of those rehab centers to see for myself. This particular center catered to the Medicare customers. The waiting room was lined with rows of seats like the ones you see in bus stations and airport terminals. They were filled to capacity with elderly people, some of them with heating pads over their backs, and some socializing around a side table laden with cookies and pots of coffee.

"Why are these people waiting here without getting their treatment?" I asked the receptionist. "Oh, don't worry about them. They only come for the coffee and the cookies," she replied. Then she immediately explained, "We do give them the heating pads".

"But they can do that as well at their homes," I said.

When I asked one patient why he doesn't use the exercise machines in the center, he told me that he tried them, but they didn't help.

"Then, why do you still come here?" I had to ask.

"It's a habit, I guess," he said. "Besides, this is an outlet for me to get out of the house. They give me transportation, coffee and cookies, and it doesn't cost me a penny."

"But who pays for all that?" I asked.

"Medicare of course," was his answer.

"Do you know how much this center is billing for their services?" I resumed.

"I don't know for sure," he said. "But I noticed one time that they were paid a few hundred dollars for therapy that I didn't have."

"Doesn't this bother you?" I reasoned with him.

"No." he said unapologetically.

71

I became a patient in one rehab center when I experienced a disabling back pain. My doctor recommended physical therapy. The manager/owner of the center I was referred to explained up front that my insurance would pay for eight visits. After three visits, I found out that the therapist was repeating the same routine that I could as well do it myself at home. I stopped going to the center but continued my exercise at home. She telephoned to encourage me to come back. "You have to make use of the rest of your allowed visits," she reasoned with me. But I knew what she really meant: I am denying her the income from the five remaining visits.

A completely opposite experience happened when a conscientious therapist was sent to my home following back surgery. After three sessions, she admitted that I could easily do the exercises she recommended by myself. We agreed that Medicare money should not be wasted on either of us; it should be saved for the patients who needed more help than me. And her services were accordingly discontinued.

Different rackets abound. A dentist, from all people, called me one day, on the advice of a friend of mine, with a business proposition. He offered to refer compensation cases for my review. All I had to do was see these patients, write medical reports and get paid. I accepted his offer and I started getting these patients.

Soon enough, a patient came to my office accompanied by her lawyer who insisted on being present while I examined her. I objected to his presence, and I evaluated her condition without any bias. At the end of the visit, he wanted me to put some specific additions to my report, but I refused. I thought that I could handle lawyers, and this incident didn't bother me until the day I was confronted by a gangster-looking man who asked me to sign a report for a patient I didn't see. "Doc, you don't have to do a thing. Just sign here and you will get paid," he said.

Needless to say, I immediately called the entrepreneurial Dentist to count me out of his program.

The truth of the matter is that everybody is abusing the system. The patients consume the service if it is for free, that is, to them as they erroneously think. The providers make money if they can get away with it. All it takes in the case of the rehab centers is a doctor who is willing to certify the need for these services every month, and the presence of entrepreneurs who know where the money is and how to get it. But most of all, the ultimate culprit is an irresponsible consumer who doesn't understand that nothing is for free and that all of us are paying for this abuse. And the 'non-therapy' continues indefinitely.

I discovered later on that there were significant numbers of similar outfits with their own lawyers, doctors, money handlers, and Mafia-type

73

connections. All of them were taking a slice of the pie. And if you want to learn how to milk the system and get your own slice, professional advisers are there to help you. They openly advertise and hold seminars on how to maximize your income.

I knew a son of a friend of mine who happened to be married to a Chiropractor. He managed his wife's business until he became well versed in all aspects of the Chiropractic practice. He then started his own business educating Chiropractors on how to make more money. His workshops became so successful that he expanded his teaching to the medical and the dental professionals.

My wife, who is a Dentist, and I had the privilege of receiving a free private lesson from him when we were visiting with his family. Listen to him speaking.

"You have to think of every new patient who walks into your office as a source of a certain amount of money. (His figure at the time was $1000.) Your job is to get those one thousand dollars. First you have to do more testing and procedures even if the patient's condition doesn't warrant them. Then you have to bring the patient back and back for more treatments and procedures. If it takes bribing your receptionist, then give her a commission if the patient does come back. Don't forget to send birthday cards to the patients and Christmas gifts to your referring doctors."

He traveled all over the country preaching his message until he made so much money that he ultimately retired in a very short time, and his wife didn't have to practice her profession any longer.

What is there in money that makes some people do anything to accumulate their millions? What is it that drives the greedy to want more and more millions? I am not against people making money, but I am only trying to expose these greedy parasites that have nothing to do with patient care but are draining our resources for their own enrichment and robbing us of precious dollars that should be rightfully spent on the care of our sick patients.

Technology

Caring for the sick is not a cost-management exercise, nor should it be. Some analytical observers name technology as a major factor in the inflated expense of our health care. I beg to differ. I'll explain that later, but for now, let me emphasize that nothing should be spared to save a human life or lessen the pain and suffering. That's what we mean when we talk about health care, i.e. preserving the health of our people. It might take a doctor, a hospital, a drug, and yes, advanced technology to accomplish that. Isn't this what it's all about?

'The best medical care in the world" did not become the best but for the innovative technological marvels. We are fortunate to live following the age of vaccines, antibiotics, running water, and a better understanding of healthier habits. Infections are not the dominant killers now. Our major killers are cancers, heart attacks, and accidents. It makes sense to direct our resources towards eliminating these afflictions as we had done with the microorganisms. As it turned out, fighting infections was relatively easy, and cheap. On the other hand, fighting the killers of our modern era is not that simple or cheap. It takes a lot of expensive technology to win this fight. That's the nature of the beast and the reality of the war.

The problems that presently face the undeveloped countries, and our own country a few generations ago, are not really health care problems. They are more political, economic, and cultural ones that have to do with the availability, or not, of clean running water, proper sewage system, and the perversity of poverty and ignorance. They are not amenable to health care reform no matter how much technology is made available. I knew that in Egypt. In Egypt, similar to other underdeveloped countries, less than life-threatening conditions had to take a second seat to the more pressing health problems like parasitic infections that drained the blood out of patients, infant diarrheas with its subsequent dehydration and fatal outcomes, the lack of immunization against preventable diseases that claimed a large number of children and shamefully raised the infant mortality rates, and many more endemic problems that didn't leave much to be given to what I call 'individual luxuries.' Moreover, the scourges of old age, like cancer, heart attacks and degenerative diseases, were less of a concern as the shortened life expectancy resulted in the decrease in the size of the potential pool for these afflictions. Contrast that with the current situation in America; the underdeveloped countries' luxuries became our necessities. And they required more technology to deal with.

Historically, wars progressed from the fist to the sword to the bullet to the canon to the tank, and ultimately to the atomic bomb and missiles. The fist didn't cost a penny, while the bomb and missiles cost hundreds of billions. Nobody suggested economizing on these weapons of war. If we considered them essential for our survival, we should consider technological advances as equally essential for our health. If wars would have killed us all, but left a pair, life would have had started again. Isn't that what happened with Noah? However, without medical advances, the majority of us would have still survived, though not to our potential longevity. But what quality of life would we have gained?

The logic is obvious. As we do not spare any expense to defend our country, we should neither spare any expense to enhance our health. Our survival depends on both, and here lies the value of technology, in war and in health.

Our afflictions are not that simple any more. It will take innovation, research, and technology to make our lives worth living. There is a lot more needed to improve our hygiene, environment, habits, and nutrition, which

I will discuss in the last chapter. But here, I will limit my discussion to the possibility of saving money if we use technology wisely.

Even if the cost is a factor, and I have already made the point that it should not be, we still can benefit from technology with manageable cost.

When the CT scans and the MRIs first came to the market, I was approached to invest in a freestanding facility. At that time, only hospitals owned these machines, but profiteering entrepreneurs saw a windfall in this technology. A new industry was thus born, the freestanding imaging centers, and the floodgates were opened. In my small town alone, there existed more than four of these centers in addition to the standard facilities in our two hospitals. And an investment proposal came my way.

This proposal was in the form of what is called limited partnership, where 35 partners buy a share each, usually with borrowed bank money, sit at home and collect sizable profit. Of course, there are risks, but the tax incentives afford you a comfortable cushion. I took the bait and made money like every other parasite on the fringe of health care. In just a couple of years, I regained my original capital and much more in profit. Was I comfortable with this arrangement? Of course; I liked the easy money. Did I make unnecessary referrals? I certainly did. Did I feel guilty? Some, but not enough to force me out of this investment until the introduction of a new law that put some restrictions on this type of investment and convinced me to reevaluate my unintended lapse of ethical judgment. The law did not forbid this type of investment. It only required making it known to consumers who were referred to a facility where the doctor had an interest in it. I chose to sell my share as I knew, by then, the entailed ethical hazards. Of course other investors were happy to buy me out and reap continuous profits.

We do need scanners, MRIs, and all the other technological marvels. But I know from personal experience that technology can cost us less if we took the greed out of the equation. Investors had made tons of money from exorbitant fees from the abuse of technology. A year or two is still all that it takes to recoup the value of the initial investment, and thereafter, it's all gravy. This is not like the touted incentive to encourage research and development, but merely a continuous money-making process.

I have already mentioned examples in my field of Otolaryngology where sinus complaints are treated with repeated courses of antibiotics and other medications that actually cost hundreds of dollars more than a diagnostic CT scan. The scan can make an early diagnosis that saves the patient pain, unnecessary suffering, and expense. The same is true for any other diagnostic or therapeutic procedure, (mammograms are an obvious example,) which might seem costly at the start, but is actually cost effective in the long run.

I will never tire from repeating: The same technology that made our health care better could be used in a frugal way to make our cost affordable. The waste is not inherent in the technology itself, but in its overuse and abuse. We should celebrate the marvels of our advanced technology, but we should demand its proper and wise use.

We have seen that the malpractice threat is a big factor in the overuse of technology. I need to add here that defensive medicine starts as that; defensive medicine, but ultimately it establishes itself as a means of making more money by adopting these same defensive practices as the standard of care. And there is always more money to be made. Every headache doesn't warrant an MRI. Every sinus "infection" shouldn't trigger a CT scan. Our standard of care should be based on better clinical sense and more sensible approach than the fear of malpractice.

I have also made it clear that consumerism and advertisement are other factors in the abuse and the overuse of technology. Marketing is conditioning the patients to demand these drugs and procedures, and profit is enticing doctors to use them more and more. This other vicious cycle has to be interrupted too.

We should not kill the goose (technology) that lays the golden eggs (better health care), but we should eliminate the vultures, inside the health care delivery system or on its fringes, that destroy this precious goose.

Placebo Effect

It is true: placebo can have the same beneficial effects as the real thing. We're not surprised to find out that, quite often, a sugar pill competes favorably with a chemical drug. However, it is certainly surprising when a sham operation proves to be as beneficial as a real one.

Let's start with the surgical placebo.

Margaret Talbot of the New York Times magazine wrote a revealing article on this and other works on the placebo effect. She started her article with this story that I quote here.

Dr. J. Bruce Mosley, the team physician for the Houston Rockets, did a double-blind study at the Houston Veterans Affairs Medical Center in 1994 with the approval of the institutional review board at Baylor and the human-studies bodies at the V. A. From a pool of ten patients, he did the standard arthroscopic surgery with the required scraping and rinsing of their knee joints on two, rinsing alone on three, and a sham operation (skin incision only) on five. None of the ten patients knew if they had the real operation or the fake one. All of them reported beneficial effects from their surgeries.

I wasn't surprised when I read this report. I had my own doubts about the benefits of arthroscopic knee surgery especially that hundreds of thousands of procedures were performed since the scope and the technique became available when many fewer cases were done prior to that. What happened to our injured knees before the introduction of arthroscopic surgery? Logically, nature designed our joints with cushioning cartilage for a reason. What happens when we remove this cartilage? We essentially remove this safety cushion, and damage to the joint will surely occur in the long run. In fact, disabling arthritis is a late complication from this surgery. But, who would remember his surgery years after the fact when the side effects would have developed?

Remember the story of the ENT surgeon who operated on patients with normal CT scans for the alleged goal of relieving their headaches? I mentioned him in a previous chapter to illustrate a fraudulent practice. You can see now that it also, inadvertently, illustrates the surgical placebo effect we are talking about. That doctor was actually and deliberately depending on the placebo effect to get rich. However, tragically and unconscionably, he didn't get the approval of any ethical committee similar to what the more honorable Dr. Mosley did.

My lack of surprise from the obvious placebo effect in surgical procedures dates back to my residency years. In fact, a study in my specialty of Otolaryngology was conducted in Europe more than thirty years ago for the same reason: To see if there was a placebo effect from one of our surgical procedures that had become "a standard and accepted medical practice."

At that time, the Endolymphatic Shunt operation (see below) was introduced for the treatment of Meniere Disease. Meniere Disease afflicts a lot of people with dizziness, buzzing in the ears, and progressive hearing loss. The accepted theory of the cause of this disease is the overproduction of fluid in tiny inner ear channels, called the semicircular canals, which monitor our movements and positions, and, in coordination with the brain, the eyes, and the muscles and bones, control our balance. (Remember that this is only a theory and is not yet established as a fact.)

On this basis, the Endolymphatic Shunt operation became the logical thing to do. In this operation, a tiny plastic tube is inserted in a part of the inner ear labyrinth, called the Endolymphatic Sac, to shunt the Endolymphatic fluid into the space surrounding the brain, which is bathed with another fluid, called Cerebrospinal Fluid (CSF). One of our astronauts had this operation done on his ear before he went to space, and the operation became a standard medical practice.

I was still a resident when this operation was introduced for the treatment of Meniere Disease. When I questioned one of my attending surgeons, who was an authority on this operation, on how it could possibly work when we were shunting a low-pressure system with microscopic quantities of fluid into a high-pressure and larger volume system, he was at a loss for an explanation. I knew at that time that even surgery could have had a placebo effect. Then, the European study came to confirm my legitimate doubts.

Europeans reported on a double-blind study similar to the one used by Dr. Mosley. They performed the real operation on half of their patients, and a sham one on the other half where they made skin incisions and removed only the superficial layers of the mastoid bone behind the ear. All patients did equally well. Europeans already knew about the placebo effect of some procedures in the seventies but we had to wait until 1994 for Dr. Mosley to open our eyes on this fact.

The Endolymphatic Shunt operation is still performed today. It is a major operation that has a substantial risk for CSF leakage around this shunt and possible meningitis-like infection. This called for some entrepreneurial surgeons to perform only the sham operation and package it in a new name; they called it 'decompression of the endolymphatic sac' where more bone is removed until the endolymphatic sac is exposed and theoretically decompressed into the mastoid cavity. In other words, they did a bigger sham operation.

A patient who is suffering the ravages of disease would happily consent to any treatment, whether medical or surgical, real or placebo, if his doctor sold it to him and if our imperfect science of medicine told him that nothing more could be offered to him.

Of course, this placebo effect is more known and more documented in the case of drugs. In fact, any new drug is rigorously investigated not only for its safety, but also for its effectiveness compared to a placebo.

Critical analysis will show that the majority of what ails us is due to minor problems and only a small number is due to life threatening or disabling conditions. This fact opens the door for a flood of drugs that, if not needed or are not effective, they might work as placebo in the time that the patient would get better anyway. I do not belittle the miraculous advances of our modern medicine, but I have to stress, again, that most of the accomplishment towards better health should be credited to better hygiene, balanced nutrition, cleaner environment, preventive medical care, better education and, where it was possible, reduction of poverty, not to the majority of the drugs we use.

Our pharmaceutical giants are making unprecedented profits by suffocating us with more and more drugs. There is no question that some of these wonder drugs are real wonders. But, when the push is for drugs that target our minor ailments, then we should think twice about their claim. I always wonder why the commercials for drugs are mostly for the latter category. You don't see commercials for digitalis, insulin, antiarrythmia drugs or chemotherapeutic agents. Most of the advertising is for antihistamines from Claritin to Zyrtec, antacids from Prilosec to Zantac and Nexium, (remember, the purple pill?) anti-diarrhea, anti-constipation, anti erectile dysfunction and anti everything you can think of. The fact is that the really beneficial drugs are used whether they advertise them or not, and they use advertisement to sell the ones that are not necessary to begin with. This is the placebo effect at its profit-making best.

Waste

Go to any operating room and see how many gloves are discarded, how many packages are opened, thoughtlessly, and subsequently thrown in the garbage without being used, how many expensive items are thrown away, and how many resources are wasted. Go to any hospital and see the loads of trash that are carted away.

Angioplasy is a procedure that opens blocked arteries of the heart (the coronary arteries) by threading a long catheter through an accessible groin artery. The manufacturer of these catheters recommends their use for one time only. Thoughtful doctors discovered that they could sterilize these catheters after each use and reuse them again with appreciable savings and without harm to their patients. But when newspaper and TV reports sensationalized this "dangerous" practice, all hell broke loose. Not surprisingly, the manufacturer was the most vociferous objector to this attempt at combating waste.

Indeed, we are a wasteful society. Our throwaways can feed, clothe and care for millions of other people who are in a dire need of the items we unnecessarily discard. We are equally a generous people who are the first to send help to disaster areas all over the world. Both waste and generosity are signs of our hard-earned affluence. And both can be controlled and properly channeled. Waste is idiotic and should be controlled. Generosity is commendable, but it should be channeled to the needy for whom it is actually intended and not to the profiteering middlemen. But this is another story not pertinent to our present discussion.

The late William Safire, the distinguished writer of The New York Times, once wrote an op-ed article on this very subject. Rummaging through his closet, he discovered tens of unused shirts, besides other things whose existence he wasn't even aware of. After a lengthy discussion about how much we buy and how much we accumulate, he concluded by mentioning his trip to the mall, which ended, guess what, by buying another shirt!

But this is not the waste I am talking about. It is in fact a small waste, but it adds up. In any event, this type of waste is what I call "benign" waste – it adds up to our cost, but it doesn't harm the patient. I am more concerned here with wasteful medical practices that we take for granted and never question their value despite the fact that they might endanger the safety of the patients or adversely increase our cost. Let me start with allergy.

Allergy injections are supposed to immunize the patient against what he is allergic to. The patient is tested for all known allergenic substances. If he reacts positively to any of these allergens, he is injected with increasing doses of the allergenic serum over a period of one to two years at increasingly longer intervals. With these injections, he is supposed to build his own acquired immunity. These injections are not without danger; minor and even serious reactions do occur.

I saw many patients who had been receiving allergy injections for years and years, and sometimes, for a lifetime. Strangely enough, all of them were still also receiving antihistamines and sometimes, steroids. This obviously meant that their allergy injections were not working. Patients thought that they were getting benefits (the placebo effect?) from these injections, and doctors knew that they were making money out of this wasteful practice.

I tried to put my theory to the test when I started my own practice. I inherited a large number of patients who were on allergy injections, some for many years. For the majority of them, judging by the cost/benefit equation, I advised against the continuation of these injections. To my great surprise, all of them followed my advice and most of them improved without the allergy injections.

This is one example of the waste I am talking about, and I'll give you more.

I was called to see a patient on consultation. His primary care doctor told me that the patient had fever of unknown origin and had developed a swelling of his face which might had been from a sinus infection that had possibly caused this fever. However, when I saw the patient, I immediately realized that the swelling was due to an abscess at the root of one of his teeth that caused his cheek to become puffy. By then, the patient had been in the hospital for a few days and had been seen by the infectious disease specialist and many other consultants in addition to undergoing extensive "battery of tests." I inserted a needle in this abscess and aspirated some pus. His swelling immediately subsided to a great extent and his pain was alleviated. I advised his doctor to discharge him with the appropriate antibiotics and send him to his own dentist. All that happened after the unnecessary waste of money and resources.

The problem here is not only waste, but also the new medical culture that replaced the proper clinical sense of listening to and examining the patient by the dependence on tests and more specialization. I mentioned in this story the infectious disease specialist who, not surprisingly, had missed this abscess as badly as the primary care doctor had.

A bright infectious disease specialist headed the infectious disease department in my hospital. One time, I teased him by saying that his specialty was redundant: any doctor can prescribe the antibiotics he himself prescribes. He responded by telling me that most of the other doctors he dealt with had no idea on how to use antibiotics!

Even in underdeveloped countries like Egypt, where infectious diseases have a major impact on health care, all doctors, regardless of their ultimate specialty, were taught and knew how to treat infections. Of course, the explosion of medical knowledge contributed to this narrow specialization, but basic knowledge is basic knowledge that should be easily mastered by all doctors no matter what specialty they happen to practice. It doesn't take a genius to know that to diagnose any infection a culture and sensitivity test is needed. According to its result, the appropriate antibiotic is prescribed. Of course, the malpractice threat forces doctors to seek the help of many specialists unnecessarily just for the sake of protecting themselves from possible future liability if anything would go wrong. Even with these considerations, there is still too much waste in ordering too many tests, in calling for too many consultants and in performing questionable procedures.

Poor training, defensive medicine, greed or whatever the reasons are behind these practices, must be addressed by any health care system to control the wasteful use of our resources and manpower. The following story is not by any means atypical.

One day, I was called to see a patient in the hospital. The reason for this consultation is not the issue here. When I introduced myself to the patient, he yelled at me, "Who the hell are you?" When I explained to him who I was and why I was called to see him, he continued in his angry belligerence. "I don't care who you are," he said. "Too many doctors have seen me since I came to this hospital. I don't understand why and to what purpose they see me. Can't you all sit down together and solve my problem instead of bothering me every day?"

I knew that he was absolutely right. I also knew that consultations and referrals are part of modern medical practice induced by the fear of malpractice as I have mentioned just now, but I also knew that they are not devoid of the profit motive. It is not unusual for a hospital patient to have a sizable number of consultants seeing him almost daily and not all of them are really necessary for his care.

Even if the help of a consultant is needed, his services are supposed to be for his opinion only. The attending physician has the responsibility to listen to his consultant and follow his advice if he accepts it. This is not what's happening. There are not only too many consultants for every hospital patient, but also, strangely enough, each consultant keeps on seeing the same patient every day, and of course, bills for these visits. I honestly believe that the fear of malpractice has nothing to do with this wasteful practice.

And there are more examples of wasteful practices.

It is not unusual to see patients in hospitals, and especially in the ICUs, getting daily x-rays and blood studies. I am not talking here about studies that are necessary when the clinical condition of the patient changes and warrants them, but I am talking about the routine repetitive studies that are ordered when there is no logical or clinical need for them. Daily chest x-rays for pneumonia! Daily blood counts for infections! What a waste. What happened to the stethoscope, the temperature chart and the clinical sense?

Pre-surgical testing, where preparatory studies are done on outpatient basis prior to the scheduled surgery to detect and correct any unforeseen abnormalities that might interfere with the surgery, is an excellent idea. But our standard of care, or longstanding habits, make us ask for a battery of tests whether needed or not. Some hospitals recognized the unnecessary waste and are starting to require pre-surgical tests only if the medical condition of the patient required them. This is a step in the right direction even if cost cutting is the inducement to this change.

Our health care system is also burdened by a different kind of costly waste. Until a few years ago, hospital personnel consisted of doctors, nurses, and a small administrative staff. Contrast that with the explosion of the number of workers who roam the corridors of our present-day hospitals. New departments sprouted out especially after the advent of managed care - the Quality Assurance Department, the Risk Management Department, the Public Relations Department, the Infection Control Department, the Case Management Department, the Home Care Department, just to mention a few. When doctors and nurses were the only ones needed for hospital patient-care, our hospitals ran smoothly and the doctor-nurse-patient relationship was intact. Compare that with what is happening now: too many paramedical hospital-employees who actually create more paper work, (remember, professionals create more work for themselves as I have illustrated in a previous chapter?) and overwhelm the doctors, and especially the nurses, with record keeping that takes them away from their primary responsibility to the patients.

This bureaucratic army,(remember also that what we are talking about here are private entities and not government,) arose with the good intension of cutting cost, but it incidentally added more cost, and at the same time did not add anything to the quality of care if it didn't actually make it worse. This is not more obvious than in the case of the Utilization Review, (UR) industry.

Utilization Review companies came into being to cut down on unnecessary medical practices like hospital admissions and length of stay. They actually did a good job and saved a lot of money, only for the insurance companies, but at an astronomical expense and a not-too-small personal profit. In 1992, over 300 UR companies were in business and their numbers increased since, Listen to what they had accomplished.

The inspector of the U.S. Health and Human Department found that in 1990 UR companies had possibly saved $1.4 million for Medicare by eliminating unnecessary cataract surgery, but at a cost of $13.3 million in fees! It is obscene to know that cost management companies are reaping income of over ten billion dollars. (The figure I came across was nine billion in 1993.) Multiply this figure by the number of other paramedical industries and you would be staggered to realize that billions of dollars are unconscionably wasted on parasitic profiteers rather than rightfully spent on the care of sick patients.

All these new industries increased our health care employment to ridiculous levels. According to the Bureau of Labor Statistic, health-care related occupations were leading all other occupations in growth during the last decade. The 43 percent increase in health care employment that was reported in 1992 does not mean that we have more doctors and nurses. We don't. Neither does it mean that the country enjoys a better health care system. It doesn't.

If this waste of manpower is not enough, think of the wasted money when you discover that billing for medical services, for instance, has become more profitable than providing the care itself as more and more doctors and hospitals are hiring 'medical billing' companies just to relieve themselves from the hassle of medical billing.

And there are more examples of waste as in the case of the freestanding surgical centers (Ambulatory Surgicenters) that sprouted up all over the map in the eighties for the understandable reason of cutting hospital costs and delivering more efficient care. Not a bad idea.

Partnerships of wealthy individuals and groups of investors capitalized on these centers, which are continuing to proliferate and are basically for-profit. Nothing is wrong with that. They do cut down on our cost for comparable care, but at what price? A few years ago, the daily newspaper of Long Island (Newsday) revealed misuse, abuse, and even dangerous practices that actually injured and even caused death to some patients at these ambulatory centers. They are not equipped to handle serious complications from the presumed minor surgeries that are performed in them.

When dealing with human beings, there is no such thing as a "minor procedure." Anything can go wrong even in the simplest operations. You should have back-up services to deal with these complications when they happen to occur.

Savings aside, I see hidden waste in these ambulatory centers from the resulting over-use, the duplication of services and the diversion of health care money to reward investors who have nothing to do with patient care. I can also foresee a danger when they would ultimately threaten the survival of our hospitals, which are already strained under low insurance reimbursement, low occupancy rates and increased overhead. If this trend continued, many of our hospitals would close and then even these ambulatory centers would not have the luxury of back-up services to care for their patients when complications are bound to arise.

The tragic fact of our wasteful culture can't be more glaring than in the so-called "alternative medicine". When we realize that billions and billions of dollars (the last figure I am aware of is 20 billion dollars a year,) are wasted on this culture every year, we have to stop and ask. "What are we doing?"

Back in Egypt, we used to sarcastically call excessive vitamin prescribing as the "vitamin therapy of the Middle East". Every patient would usually get prescriptions for his necessary medications, then more prescriptions for all types of vitamins and tonics. It was not uncommon for patients to ask for more vitamins and for doctors, whether willingly or just to please their patients, to prescribe them. Strangely enough, the well nourished and the well fed were the ones who insisted on more vitamins.

The clock has turned a full circle, backwards. Here we are in the best nourished and the most scientific county in history, and we practice this wasteful illogical consumption. The shamans and the witches have returned with a vengeance.

Remember how we discovered the essential vitamins? Our seafaring ancestors roamed the oceans for months without fresh food. When they developed bleeding from their gums, they called it scurvy and blamed it on evil spirits. They soon realized that it wasn't due to evil spirits, but to lack of vitamin C, which was abundant in fresh fruits and vegetables. They subsequently ate fresh fruits and vegetables and cured their scurvy. All other deficiencies were ultimately traced to other items of food, and one by one all other vitamins became known as well as the foods that supplied them. The cures to their deficiencies were not pills, but the proper food. Sadly enough, packaged herbs, vitamins, and tonics are forced

99

on us when all of them are abundant in our normal diet. Entrepreneurs packaged food and sold it to us in the form of expensive pills, more so if the label said 'organic.'

The scientific discipline is what took us to the moon and gave us the present miracles of modern medicine. It is a pity that we allowed a huge industry to flourish and drain our resources by this so-called "alternative medicine".

A recent report from the Institute of Medicine, a branch of the National Academy of Science, concluded that large doses of vitamins and antioxidants are not only useless in preventing chronic diseases, but might also be harmful. A recent and similar study showed that gingko beloba proved to be ineffective in enhancing memory. These reports also emphasized that Americans already get enough nutrition from the food they eat. Did we have to wait for a study like this one to tell us the obvious?

The beginning of this travesty started when the cost of our medial care escalated to unmanageable levels and more money was poured into health care. However, instead of reforming the system, we dismantled it by empowering the HMO's and humiliating the doctors. Everybody became a doctor without the requirement of education or license. The pie was so huge and everybody wanted his piece. New fads invaded our culture and the stage was ripe for the profit. The indoctrination was so successful that mainstream medicine took a defensive stand. Under severe pressure, more and more insurance companies were forced to cover this new discipline. Even our congress bent over under pressure from lobbyists and joined in the chorus. Look for more waste.

How could we be duped to that extent? What had happened to our logic and scientific belief in evidence? How could we allow a fringe industry to siphon billions of dollars from our health care budget for their profit and to our detriment? This is certainly the ultimate waste

Death is Natural

Our modern life has pushed us to the extreme of anxiety. Worrying about the next bill to pay, the next buck to make and the next pleasure to experience had made the tomorrow a distant future that we forgot that life has to end sometime. And the miracles of modern science and medicine didn't help. "You're telling me that we went to the moon and you can't help me?" This is what we hear when we tell our patients that we can't solve a particular problem. We are also frequently asked to "do something" when faced with a terminal illness, as if doing something would prevent the inevitable. We became doers and didn't learn when to stop.

Late in a cold winter evening, I was called to the emergency room where a patient of mine was "bleeding from her neck". I immediately recognized her when the ER nurse mentioned her name.

She was a woman in her mid-forties who had been under my care for the previous few years. The first time I saw her, she was complaining of a sore throat. Even with her history of smoking and drinking, I was surprised to discover, at her age, a tumor in her gum. Biopsy proved it to be cancerous but, fortunately, it was a small one that was treated by radiation with excellent results. She failed to return for her follow up, and apparently, as I discovered later on, she continued to smoke and drink.

She returned after a year with another tumor in the back of the tongue that was extensive and needed radical surgery. I had to remove half of her tongue, part of her jaw, and the lymph nodes of her neck. Recent techniques in reconstructive surgery by vascularized flaps (borrowing tissues from nearby areas with their own blood supply), enabled me to put her back together, and she looked pretty close to normal. Only then did she stop smoking and drinking, but it was too late.

In another year, a third tumor appeared on her vocal cords. Total laryngectomy (removal of the voice box) was necessary, and she lost another part of her body. Unfortunately, this was not the end of her story.

A fourth tumor appeared in the tonsil on the other side of her throat. This time surgery was not possible; there were no more healthy tissues around the tumor to make its removal feasible. Previous radiation precluded further use of this mode of treatment. Chemotherapy was the only option left.

She did not respond to chemotherapy, and her tumor continued to grow until it reached the neck and ultimately broke through the skin. A fistula, (communication between the throat and the neck) developed with saliva pouring out of it. There was nothing else to do except lesson her suffering and control her pain.

A sickening feeling overtook me when I received the emergency room call on that fateful night. The tumor must have had eroded the big artery of the neck (the Carotid artery), I surmised.

When I reached the emergency room, my patient was lying on a stretcher in a pool of blood and pale as a ghost. My suspicions were correct. It was indeed a carotid blow out. "Do something," her boyfriend pleaded with me. He was understandably voicing the 'do something' mentally of our culture. In turn, I obliged by reflexive actions; I applied pressure against the artery and rushed her to the operating room.

In the operating room, the anesthesiologist pumped a few units of blood in her veins until I managed to tie the bleeding artery. I knew that in doing so, half of her brain might die. When she woke up, it was apparent that she had indeed suffered the expected stroke and lost the function of half of her body. Thankfully, she died a few days later.

I treated another patient with a long history of smoking and drinking, but this time with an advanced tumor of the back of her tongue. When I advised a commando procedure (removal of half of the tongue, part of the jaw, neck muscles, lymph nodes and the big vein of the neck) with little chance of cure, she understandably refused to submit to this horrendous operation. Radiation was the other less effective option.

She received a full course of radiation, but the tumor came back. The commando operation was the only option left, and this time she wanted it done despite the fact that all of her tongue might go as well as her voice box. A second opinion from an eminent surgeon in the big city agreed and she consented to have the surgery done.

When I tried to save half of her tongue during the operation, I found that it was impossible to do so and get around the tumor, which was more massive than my studies had shown, as is usually the case with tongue tumors especially after radiation. The surgery was a success, but she was left as a cripple without a tongue or larynx. She couldn't swallow or talk. Her family wanted her to love and she didn't want to die.

She survived for a few more months, but her cancer returned and gradually broke through the skin. Chemotherapy added more to her misery, but did not touch the tumor. The merciful death ultimately ended her suffering.

The American part of me felt detached and even proud in my ability to do this "beautiful" operation. I even received money for doing it, gave a talk about it in a medical meeting with slides and all, and gained a reputation for being an eminent Head and Neck Surgeon.

The Egyptian side of me, on the other hand, gave me sleepless nights thinking about the meaning of life, the reality of death, and the mystery behind the human existence. I donated the money I received form the insurance company to the hospice unit of my hospital where my patient received her terminal care. (Hospice was a new discipline at that time, and I believed in its philosophy.)

Never in my life had I ever faced the complex issue of death than when I went through those two experiences. What is it that makes people cling to life with this tenacity? What is it that drives us, the caregivers, to exercise our knowledge and abilities to add misery to our patients who are already unfortunate to have life ending diseases? What is it that makes us fear death when most of us are religious and believe in heaven and the after life?

Life has certain attributes without which living has no meaning or value. We kill animals for food because we reason, in addition to our survival need, that they don't think, feel, or know what life is. On the other hand, we rightfully care for the blind, the deaf, and the disabled because they are functioning human beings who have the right, and are capable, to enjoy their lives. Strangely enough, we spend a lot of resources on extending the lives of people whose terminal illness robs them of the faculties that we define as necessary for a dignified life and suffer through it too.

The miracles of modern medicine should be used to improve the quality of our lives, not to prolong the process of dying. The "do something" culture should be realistic enough to know when to stop the "doing". Nature has a scheme with its own laws and rules. We know that change and evolution are the only constant attributes of life. What has a beginning must have an end. The issue should not be how to extend life, but how to make the available life worth living and enjoyable.

Like everyone else, I couldn't help but notice the increasing numbers of people living to old age. In fact, they were the majority in my practice, and their numbers increased steadily over the years. As much as I value the beauty and the optimism of the young, I learned to see the beauty of old age with its wisdom and fulfillment, despite the wrinkles and the physical weaknesses. That's why I feel sorrow and defeat when my elderly patients tell me that there is no fun in the "golden years", or when some of them say "they kill horses, don't they".

Don't be fooled by statistics. If more of us do live longer, statistics don't tell us what the figures really mean and they don't tell us what to expect when we cross the line to that 'Promised Land' of the golden age. How many of our elderly are on respirators or in nursing homes, or vegetating somewhere with Alzheimer's, mental deficiencies or loneliness and poverty? Many others like them are counted as "alive". I am certainly not advocating, "Kill the horse." There would be no place for assisted suicide or euthanasia if we let nature takes its merciful course and purpose without interference from our brutal technology when it is used to prolong the dying process.

One day I received a call form a nursing home to see a patient who was bleeding from around his tracheotomy tube. Knowing that I couldn't possibly handle this bleeding in the nursing home when his doctor had told me that he suspected an erosion of the big artery of the neck, I advised transferring the patient to the ER. I expected the worst as soon as I had recognized who that patient was. How could I ever forget him?

Eight years earlier, I was called to see him in the hospital because of difficulty swallowing and breathing in addition to aspiration and frequent pneumonia. His diagnosis was Lou Gherric Disease that paralyzed his body. I performed a tracheotomy to help his breathing, and removed two salivary glands (called Submandibular Glands), and ligated the ducts of the other two big salivary glands (the Parotids) to decrease the excessive saliva that produced the aspiration and the resulting pneumonia. He ended on a respirator, and stayed in the hospital for over 6 months. I presumed that he must have had died until I received that call form the nursing home 8 years later.

In the emergency room, I discovered that the bleeding was coming from ulceration around the tracheotomy tube and not from erosion of the big artery of the neck as his doctor had suspected. After a quick cauterization, the bleeding stopped and he was returned to the nursing home with his respirator, oxygen, and all the machinery of modern medicine. As sorry as I felt for him and his family, I couldn't help but think of the fallacy of the numbers when he and many others like him were added to our survival statistics.

Go to any Intensive Care Unit in any hospital in the country and see how many patients are on respirators, dialysis, life supporting drugs, and the likes. I am not talking here about the acute patients following surgeries and accidents, but about the terminally ill ones who are in different stages in the death process.

I happened to perform a large number of tracheotomies on the "prisoners" of the ICU. No follow up was required of me after that. However, I would get the charts sometime later on in the record room to sign my surgical notes. I always made a point to see for myself how many of my tracheotomised patients survived and how many of them died. No surprise, the majority of them would have had ultimately died after lengthy and costly hospitalization. In their legacy, massive medical charts would be filed in the record room.

As a physician, I find it hard to make the following statement, but someone has to: If we think twice before we interfere with the inevitable death, we can lessen the suffering of thousands of us who die each year. This is a logical and a humane imperative and not an economic one, though saving our resources for the proper care of all of us who have the potential for longer, comfortable and healthy life is as logically humane, despite the ranting of the 'death panels' crowd.

Back in the old country and in the America of a few generations back, when death-prolonging technology was not available, 'Mother Nature' took care of us. Death was accepted as a natural end to life itself. We have to realize that the availability of these technological wonders should not be construed as a license to use them unnecessarily.

The hospice philosophy started in England. It became a wonderful venue to lessen the suffering of the terminally ill, prepare them and their families for a dignified death, and decrease the delusions of magic cures and eternal life on earth. If we accept nature's dictates of the inevitable end of life, we have to expand the hospice care and be more realistic about our present determination to conquer death.

An African legend tells the story of a man who was walking in the forest when he heard a voice crying for help. Reaching the source of the voice, he discovered it to be coming from a python. "Help me and I'll do anything for you," said the python. "An ant is stuck in my throat and is going to kill me," the python pleaded with him. "But how can I help you?" The man questioned her. The python answered: "Put your hand in my throat, and get the ant out."

"You can't fool me with this. You will bite my hand and kill me," said the man. "Trust me," said the python. "I will never do that. Besides, you can always cut my head off with your machete if I tried to hurt you." The python reasoned with him and he believed her.

He stuck his hand in her throat, and sure enough he brought out the offending ant. The python was so grateful that she offered to grant him any wish he desired.

"Give me eternity." This was the man's only wish. He then added: "I don't want to die."

"I'll grant you your wish. You will get your eternity," said the python.

When the man reached his home, he covered himself and went to sleep. The next day, his family was looking for him and found him asleep under the cover. However, when they removed the cover, his body wasn't there. They found on the bed a large rock instead.

We are not stone or eternal. We are made of flesh that has to die, even if we lived for a thousand year.

Lurking Danger, Promising Hope

At the turn of the century, two well-written books were published when the health care debate was in the news as it is now and will certainly continue for years to come if we don't finalize a definitive reform. The first is titled "Mismanaged Care," written by Michael E. Makover, M.D. The other is "The Medical Racket," by the professor of social science and best-seller writer, Martin L. Gross.

Dr. Makover exposed the glaring defects of managed care in his scholarly book. He researched the subject extensively, but he reached the wrong conclusion. His critical judgment on the single payer system was superficial and unfair (this will be discussed in the last chapter). However, his favoritism for the medical saving accounts (MSA), contradicts his logical criticism of managed care.

In the MSA, patients are given a tax incentive to essentially self-insure themselves. (This is similar to the requirement included in the new bill.) They are allowed to put aside, tax deductible, a certain amount of money in a tax free savings account to be used for basic health care. But, they are required to buy coverage for catastrophic illness that carries a large deductible. If you follow this scenario and get seriously sick, you have to spend from your saving account the required deductible of the catastrophic policy before your insurance kicks in. They tell us that there is a great probability that you will not get sick every year thus your saving account will proportionately increase. I would ask for a guarantee before I buy into this scheme.

Suppose you can't afford to save in this MSA or that you have used all your savings in one bad year. Who will then pay your basic health care expense and your newly kicked-in yearly deductible? Besides, don't they realize our famously low percentage of savings or our routine and huge indebtedness?

Built in this scheme of funding is some type of bureaucracy, necessarily a government agency, to monitor these accounts, from how much is contributed to it, to how much is withdrawn, and by whom. You have to create a monstrosity of rules and regulations to monitor these accounts. And this complexity is coming from the same people who are originally against any government bureaucracy. And, you know what that breads? More bureaucracy. And more Bureaucracy means more expense and more complications.

Moreover, who will manage our catastrophic insurance premiums even if we get this no-illness guarantee? You guessed it, the same for-profit companies that both authors had judged them to be bad for us, the same for-profit companies that our congress had entrusted with that much money and the care of our patients. How would they be better managers and without bankrupting the insurance pool if they were bound to spend on more catastrophic and expensive occurrences? They would definitely raise our premiums and induce another cycle of escalating costs. Furthermore, the same free-market business rules which require a chunk of the money to be allocated to their profit, CEO compensation and their administrative bureaucracy rather than spent on the care of the patients, would necessarily apply similar to what is happening in the managed care system that the author criticized.

I tried to check on these promising MSAs. I called my medical society when they offered MSAs to their members. The administrator who answered my call explained, as I have expected, that I would have to buy a catastrophic insurance prior to becoming eligible for this MSA. He compared my cost for the freedom insurance that I had, to that of the

MSA and concluded that it was cheaper for me to keep the freedom plan. He advised against this coverage. I have to borrow Mr. Gross expression: what a racket.

Mr. Gross, true to his history of insightful critiques of political establishment, government's waste, and the medical community, resumed the exposure of the medical profession and the insurance companies. Similar to Dr. Makover, he reached another ill-conceived solution in what he called Community Medicine.

In the Community Medical Plan (CMP), Mr. Gross divides the country into five hundred small districts of 500,000 populations. He didn't say where the money would come from, though I presume that it would come from some kind of tax. If it is from local tax, how can the mobile patient carry his insurance around? If it is from a centralized tax, how much do we allocate to each district if the demographics changed as they surely would? And who would manage this money? An ill-defined "organization," i.e. another bureaucracy as the ones he condemned as a racket. The rest of the details are too complicated to make managed care inefficiencies look comparatively good. Instead of accepting a simple single payer system, he comes up with 500 districts with their own individual rules and complexities. We have known that fragmentation leads to confusion, more bureaucracy, more inequities and more expense. What a racket.

As much as both authors are against the government, their plans require government's help for both finance and regulations. Here goes this anti-government sentiment.

Someone else suggested Employer Mandated Financing (EMF), more rules, more regulations, and more uncertainty. Wouldn't the government be required to pass laws, regulate the system, and monitor its performance? How strange is it that whoever is against the government devises a plan that would certainly require more government, more fragmentation, and more confusion? How about the unemployed, the self-employed, and the people on welfare? Another racket is obviously looming, again, in this so called EMF.

Some experts devised a plan to cover all children while others concentrated on the elderly or the poor. All these are worthy ideas, but they are in fact detours to avoid the proper and the only reform needed. And what about the rest of us? We too do get sick. Helping some of the population would not do. It would actually create more bureaucracy, more confusion, and it would delay the inevitable.

Mr. Bush suggested tax credits for the uninsured to buy their own insurance. A similar proposition is included in the current congressional bill. We already know what that means.

Congress passed and President Bush signed a Medicare Prescription Drug Benefit Plan. When I calculated the cost for a senior who signs for this plan, I discovered that one has to come up with at least $700 out of pocket for deductibles and coinsurance plus the required premiums, more than $1000, each year before this coverage kicks in. This is already $1700. Even then the coverage is only for up to $2500 per year as it disappears in what is famously known as the donut hole. And who is going to be in control of this huge budget that was estimated at more than 300 billion but is now expected to exceed 500 billion? That law mandates that, not Medicare, but the same private managed care companies would control this trove of money, the same companies that have promised us, in their inception, cheaper medical care but have soon enough burdened us with higher premiums and much less care. You bet the same outcome will happen in this ill-conceived prescription drug benefit program.

Another hidden danger from all of these partial shortsighted reforms is the creation of a two-tier system where the wealthy can get the best health care and the rest of us would undoubtedly get mediocre care. There is another idea that patients should pay directly to their health care providers then get reimbursed from their insurance companies if they have coverage, with the assumption that they, the patients, would be better guardians of their own money. We tried this same system before, it was called fee-for-service, and look what we ended up with.

If that is not complicated enough, the geniuses in our congress have formulated what they call a health care reform plan. Over 2000 pages were needed to navigate through another new bill because we are still trying to avoid the single payer system, the logical, the only workable, the more economical, the much less complicated, and the simplest system to deliver the proper medical care to all of us.

Any partial reform will create its own momentum, which will make it more difficult, if not impossible, to effect any new change. Well-meaning people who support partial reform ignore the fact that, if we entrust the management of our health care money, again, to the for-profit insurance companies, these companies will use their power, influence and lobbyists to block any meaningful reform if this is found to be necessary in the future. (This is exactly what happened in 2009.) Moreover, the profiteering, the abuse and the waste will continue as well as this unresolved big money influence. We must have the courage and the foresight to solve this problem once and for all.

The stumbling block towards this goal is the word that everybody is afraid of: Government. But the fact is that we are the government. Let us see what is true, or not true, about us and about our government.

Fouad B. Michael, M.D.

Why are we afraid of the government? This is supposed to be a democracy: a government from the people and for the people. Is history reversing itself and we are allowing the few to dictate how to govern us all? Don't we have cyclical elections when we are supposed to choose the best representatives to serve us with humility and honor? How could we allow arrogant, ignorant and corrupted officials to stay in office and degrade our government as if they were not part of it? What a farce.

In the feudal system, few landowners controlled the fate of the rest of the population. The industrial revolution created wealthy industrialists who ascended to the role of the feudal lords. Communism introduced a single party that dictated what is good and what is bad. Only democracy gave the people control of their own destiny. This is what is supposed to be the ideal system. And it is if the practice fulfills the ideal.

The defects in a democracy are not inherent, but are in fact defects in its application. A democratically elected government is a reflection of the people whom it represents. We cannot avoid the responsibility and blame the government for all of its ills and ours.

When the word government comes in any discussion, we tend to view it as an evil word. There is nothing evil about the government. The evil is only the evil we allow. We are the government, and our government

120

is as good, or as bad, as all of us who have the power to elect or dismiss our representatives.

The American people are basically good sensible people. It is a glaring contradiction that when our freely elected representatives fail to work for our own common good, we turn around and say that the government is bad? We are the ones who elect our government to begin with.

The most obvious reason for this paradox is the corruption of the electoral process by big money, big special interest groups, and big political action lobbies. Still, government is our best hope to put in order our modern, complicated, and diverse society. Individual and group interests are only fodder for a jungle war in which all of us will loose. The fact remains that after we elect our representatives, they fall under the influence of lobbyists with deep pockets tempting them with contributions and help for their reelection. Therefore, election finance reform is a prelude to any other sensible reform whether in health care or in any other enterprise.

Bad government is the result of astronomical numbers of laws, rules, and regulations that our congressional geniuses keep on churning every year. The resulting bureaucracy is only the byproduct of this legislative maze. The problem is in fact not the bureaucracy but the flood of laws that created it.

Of course they are. But our representatives shouldn't justify their pay by

waking up every morning to think of new laws to modify the laws they

enacted the day before. They don't have to appoint a commission to study

a problem they are supposed to study themselves, and then appoint another

commission to study the report of the first commission.

When the idea of a flat tax rate was introduced for a sweeping tax

reform without loopholes, I jokingly told my accountant that his profession

would disappear if this idea were adopted. He laughed at my suggestion

and said that this will never happen in America. "What we describe as a

complicated tax code is intentionally used to solve social problems," he

said.

I am not an economist, nor do I know the merits of this tax proposal.

But the idea of solving social problems by a complicated tax code strikes

me as a misguided escape from facing the real issues.

For the same reason, we are doomed to face another complicated

code in health care that necessarily requires thousands of pages to satisfy

special interests that have nothing to do with health care.

Our politicians should have the courage to resolve any social issue

on its own merit without hiding behind more complicated and unworkable

solutions. I feel that there is a self-serving, though unconscious, conspiracy

Some might say that laws are necessary to organize our society.

to patch the ragged edges of any problem and leave more room for more work, more legislation, more profiteering and more power.

The critical point that all of us agree upon is that the government is our vehicle for survival like in defense and health care. Simplify the laws and limit the regulations and I guarantee you less bureaucracy and much less cost.

It is clearly obvious that fragmentation in military procurement and other public spending is a big factor in the famous $700 toilette seat. The political reality favors influential states and districts, and the financial benefits presumably create jobs and add to our common wealth. But what we really get from all of that? The $700 toilette seat and the "bridge to-no-where" are just more publicized examples of the resulting waste.

In health care, fragmentation adds more bureaucracy and creates many more hurdles to access and cost control. This is what happened when hundreds of managed care companies assumed the responsibility of our health care. They created more bureaucracy, confusing rules and regulations, and deficient care.

One payer with simple rules and a standardized system is the only logical way to deliver effective high quality care with the least expense. And the only power to administer such a system is the government. It was done in other countries and it can, and should be done here.

For-Profit Private Insurance is Not the Solution

Before the managed care era, the not–for-profit Blue Cross and Blue Shield managed to survive and actually made profit despite the fact that they paid whatever the doctors and hospitals charged and that the patients stayed longer in the hospitals. Compare that to the initial financial difficulties of the commercial companies of managed care that were going out of business, declaring bankruptcy or running out of reserves to stay solvent when their premiums were going up, reimbursement for doctors and hospitals were going down and hospital occupancy was the lowest in decades. In New York State, Oxford ran out of cash and resorted to protection under Chapter 11, and MDNY was denying services right and left. Strangely enough, that entire trend reversed as the inevitable free market rules drove premiums to unprecedented levels and brought these companies back to obscene profitability. If you want to know how much these companies are making, just think of the hundreds of millions of dollars that the Humana Corporation could afford to pay in a settlement with the government after admitting to fraud charges.

All that became possible because they doubled and tripled our premiums. However, not all that money goes to patient care. A large chunk of it goes to profit. Add to that the 30% that they keep to enrich their bureaucrats and their stock holders. Yes, the fee-for-service system created an unacceptable escalation in the cost of our health care which ultimately delivered us to the brutal world of the for-profit one. However, neither is the right direction where our health care system should take.

The managed care solution was supposed to manage the escalating health care cost and, hopefully, to improve the quality of patient care. What we got was a monstrosity of a system that, despite the lowering of our cost in the beginning, steadily increased it, and at the same time, reduced the quality of patient care. It has also created a flood of rules, regulations and paper work that choked the whole system. Remember, we are talking here about private enterprises and not the government.

Before managed care, I employed only one office worker who took care of my patients' needs and a minimum of paper work. With managed care, I needed four workers to handle the same load of patients but an astronomical increase in the paper work. And that's despite the fact that I joined only four managed care companies. I know of doctors who joined many more companies and had to hire much more help just to keep up with the resulting explosion of paper work and the confusing maze of rules and regulations.

Managed care companies slowly and methodically infiltrated the market. They started by luring doctors to join their panels and by offering them reasonable fees. At the same time, they solicited employers and subscribers with the promise of reduced premiums. The noose was in place and the strangulation began.

The initial reasonable fees for the providers gradually decreased and decreased and decreased until they reached a pitiful low level that couldn't possibly cover their overhead expenses. "We'll give you more volume of patients to make up for the reduced fees," they reassured the doctors. "You have to be more efficient," they threatened the hospitals. Try to take a complete history, then perform a thorough physical examination and decide on a plan for management and treatment. It takes a lot of precious time to properly do all of that. Here goes the increased volume. Or if you want to survive and get the increased volume, there goes the quality of care. When hospitals tried to be more efficient, the result was the drive-through deliveries, the premature discharges and the brutal efforts to cut down on the 'length of stay.' The many variables in the individual case of each patient don't even matter. This is a very risky practice indeed.

To complicate matters more, every managed care company establishes its own rules and regulations, and every company offers different policies that are governed by yet other sets of rules and regulations. This policy requires referral from a gatekeeper to see a specialist. That one doesn't. Some policies will allow yearly check up, but others will allow it only if it is deemed 'medically necessary.' This one will allow the specialist to order X rays and scans, but the other one demands prior authorization from a primary care doctor. All of them insist on pre-certification for any elective or even emergency procedure. They created a nightmare.

Just trying to obtain pre-certification becomes a tremendous hassle. You have to deal first with automated telephone messages. If..., press 1. If..., press 2. If..., press 3 and the pound key. There is no end to the numbers. If that's not enough, you can go back to the beginning of the menu. Yes, you can ultimately get to talk with a human being, but you have to hold and hold and hold. It is not unusual to stay on hold for close to an hour. My secretary tells me that she doesn't work for me anymore - she is in fact working for the insurance companies. That's partly why I needed 4 secretaries.

If you're lucky, you get the required pre-certification, but don't hold your breath. The confirmation note comes with a caveat: "This authorization does not guarantee payment after the service is done." I am not kidding, and they mean it, too. They might not pay for the service even if they authorized it beforehand! In fact, they have done that quite often, which had necessitated more telephone calls, more struggle with the same automated menu and more re-submissions. This practice is, no doubt, an intentional tactic to hold on to their money longer, or it might actually be intended to discourage the doctors from giving the needed care and, in effect, denying the patients the proper care. I suppose that it is for both reasons.

The process of pre-certification is not only an added burden on my secretaries' time, but it is also a nightmare for me. The managed care companies programmed their computers, and their reviewers for that matter, to look for specific requirements for every conceivable procedure. For example, for every septoplasty (surgery for the deviated septum) my secretary tries to pre-certify, they ask: How many times did you see this patient? Did you treat him with antibiotics, antihistamins and nasal steroids? Did you get a scan? Etc. etc.

When my secretary answers their questions guided only by the medical record, she can't possibly explain everything. In the end, I have to talk to the reviewer personally. She is usually a nurse sitting somewhere, most probably in another state, with a computer screen in front of her.

"Doctor, how many times did you see this patient?"

"I am only a specialist, and I saw this patient once, when his primary care doctor referred him to me."

"Do you know how many times his primary care doctor had seen him?"

"I know that he might have seen him for three times."

"This is not enough for us. Do you know how many antibiotics he received?"

"I know that he received three antibiotics, but antibiotics do not treat deviated septums. That's why his problem wasn't solved."

"Then how many antihistamins and nasal steroids he used?"

"Madam, antihistamines and nasal steroids are not the proper treatment for a deviated septum. This is bone and cartilage that's twisted and can be only corrected by surgery."

"Well then, did you get a scan?"

"No, the scan is not indicated in this situation. You make the diagnosis of a deviated septum by looking inside the nose. It is ultimately a visual diagnosis."

"We do require a scan for documentation."

We continue to argue endlessly.

In the end, she declares, "Well, doctor, I am not going to authorize this operation. Sorry."

If you didn't have any luck with the nurse reviewer, you probably won't have any luck either with the physician reviewer. Yes, you can appeal to him, but he is similarly programmed to follow the same menu.

When I discussed this common scenario with one of my savvy colleagues, he told me to give them what they wanted. "Just give them the answers they are programmed to look for. Bring the patient back and back. Prescribe two or three courses of antibiotics and get a scan. Let them pay for all these services even if you think that these services are not necessary. This will serve them right." That is, lie and cheat. I couldn't. As a result I lost a lot of "business" and my patients didn't get the care they deservedly needed.

This is obviously a dangerous game. If doctors lie to and cheat on their insurance companies, they would ultimately lie to and cheat on their patients and their colleagues too. The lying and cheating would become the 'standard and accepted medical practice. Actually, a recent study published in the JAMA (The Journal of the American Medical Association) detected this dangerous pattern.

When the insurance companies deny services with the excuse that the services were medically unnecessary, they take us back to the Dark Ages of medicine. Over 90% of our care is for elective, not life threatening, conditions. Our goal is a better quality of life. We educate and train doctors not only to save our lives, but also to lessen our suffering and to make our lives worth living. We entrust our doctors with this job and we should insist that nobody else interferes with their judgment. If we follow the managed care logic, we might as well close all medical schools and let the technocrats manage our care through a computer program.

Even the language is deviously used in a psychological game to condition us into a new culture intended to benefit the insurance companies. We used to communicate with each other through a simple language that referred to a doctor as doctor, a patient as patient, a hospital as hospital and so forth. Now a doctor is a health care giver. A patient is a consumer. A hospital is a health care facility. A primary care physician is a gate keeper.

Too many other words were added to the medical vernacular to the confusion of everybody. It would take me dozens of pages to enumerate and explain the meaning of those words. Just look for *capitation*. If you don't find its meaning, as used in health care, in a regular dictionary, save yourself the trouble of more investigating. But, if you are a doctor trying to make ends meet and sustain your practice, you better make sure to understand the meaning of those words and follow the confusing definitions when dealing with them.

We had enough experimentation, including this foray into the managed care wilderness. Any solution that doesn't cure the problem will ultimately and surely kill the patient. As I have made it clear before, private insurance companies are generating a momentum of their own, and it will be harder and harder, and more costly, to correct or change it. We should not play games with our sick people. We should, however, do the right thing once and for all, and very quickly before it is too late.

The Solution: A Single Payer System

A single payer system run by the government is the only way to ensure universal and cost effective coverage. Let me explain.

The absolute necessity of universal health care, if you're not convinced yet, will be clear when you happen to experience illness, pain, deformity or disability. Nothing in the world equals good health, not wealth or power, not beauty or youth, nothing. Unfortunately, sickness and pain do afflict all of us one time or another. This is a collective risk that should be addressed by a collective responsibility. Listen to what Disraeli said in 1877. "The health of the people is really the foundation upon which all their happiness and all their powers as a state depend."

If the numbers of the uninsured and the underinsured make it necessary for a universal health care system that covers us all, any new reform should also address the cost factor. If we have a limitless supply of

133

money, any system we adopt will be as good as any other even if we fail to eliminate all the fraud, the waste and the inefficiencies. But we don't have this luxury. Therefore we have to aim at the best possible health care, which we don't have, and understand how it is different than medical care, which we certainly have, for some but not all, and which we can't afford. This I'll explain later.

One more fact we should understand is that private insurance in a capitalist society can work for car and other similar types of insurance but not in health care. If the automobile insurance companies raised our premiums to stay viable and profitable, we, the consumers, would have a lot of options. We could rearrange our budgets to pay for these higher premiums. We could drive less expensive cars. We could even get rid of our cars and use public transportation. Whatever we do, we would do it as individuals and society as a whole wouldn't incur any added expense.

This is not true in health care. If your appendix is about to rupture, you don't say, "I can't afford to remove it" and let it rupture.

Unfortunately, any health care system that's controlled by the for-profit private insurance companies would allow this to happen, whether due to complicated rules and regulations, requirement for pre-certification, denial of coverage, or the resulting increase in the numbers of the uninsured. They, the private insurance companies, are in the business of making money, not to care for our ills. Yet, we have been trying to reform the system by keeping these companies in business.

Winston Churchill is claimed to have said, "You can count on the Americans to do the right thing, but not before they have tried everything else."

We have tried the fee-for-service system. It didn't work. It actually gave us a corrupted and a fraudulent system that was overly expensive and left millions without insurance or medical care.

We have also tried a managed care system to deal with one aspect of the problem, the cost, but it unexpectedly worsened the corruption, the abuse and the fraud and, in the end, the cost as well. At the same time, it didn't solve the inequities nor did it care for the uninsured whose numbers actually increased. It also added more bureaucracy, more paper work, more regulations and much less choice. The same will certainly recur with the new legislation.

We have tried the generosity of the not-for-profit organizations and the employer mandated financing, but that didn't work either. Consider the myth of the employers' financing of health care: we should be embarrassed to know that when almost all of us were working, when the unemployment was at around 5%, 44 millions of us had no health insurance and as many of us were underinsured! With over 10% of us unemployed at present how can an employer-mandate help?

Some reformers are under the illusion that Medical Savings Accounts or Community Medicine might be a solution as I explained in a previous chapter. But common sense tells us that these well-intentioned solutions wouldn't work either. As has happened with the managed care experiment, further experimentation is bound to create new monstrosities that would carry their own momentum and make it more difficult to adopt the correct reform that should be established once and for all. This is exactly what happened in the assumed reform that bogged us in 2009.

Unfortunately, we are afraid to give the responsibility for correcting the ills of our health care system to the government. But as we have trusted the government with our national defense to survive as a country, it is equally logical that we must also trust our government with our health care to survive as individuals.

This is not a marginal issue that should be left to the forces of the free market. Yes, our government is not perfect, but its imperfection should not be a reason to dismiss it as the proper vehicle for making needed social reforms. As we do for our sick people, we should also do for our government: treat the disease, not kill the patient.

One of the most honorable and most knowledgeable persons to serve in our government, and who knows more about health care than anyone else, is Joseph Califano, the secretary of HEW in the Carter administration. He wrote in his book, *America's Health Care Revolution:*

"The federal government and the states have been moving to deal with the demons of fraud, abuse and waste in Medicare and Medicaid. It's far easier to do (that) with Medicare, which is a single program operated by the federal government... Medicaid is a tougher nut to crack. It is one program but more than fifty different health plans... The millions of Medicaid transactions that occur in this complex administrative maze are prone to error, fraud and abuse."

He is essentially saying that a single federal program is better than a fragmented one run by many entities – 50 states, in the case of Medicaid. Isn't this the fragmentation that's happening in the private insurance maze? A system that allows hundreds and hundreds of private insurance companies each with its own rules and regulations and profit motive is surely more conducive to errors, fraud and abuse.

President Clinton characterized our system in the early nineties as "too uncertain and too expensive, too bureaucratic and too wasteful. It has too much fraud and too much greed." Unfortunately, this assessment is still valid.

The only logical way for definitive reform is to address the three players involved in any health care system: the patients, the doctors, (with the necessary hospitals, nurses and pharmaceutical companies,) and the payer. There is no way that we can eliminate these three players. But, we can and should eliminate all other players who are opportunistic, parasitic and unnecessary, namely, the lawyers, the for-profit insurance companies, the entrepreneurial leeches and yes, Madison Avenue.

The problem necessarily begins with the presence of patients. Until we understand all the secrets of life, patients will be here to create this problem. The obvious way to start with is to decrease the numbers of patients by adequate research to find the causes of our ills and prevent them. Yes, prevention is the inescapable goal we have to pursue.

The same Joseph Califano wrote another book, *Radical Surgery,* in which he touched on every conceivable aspect of disease prevention. We should heed his authoritative advice. His conclusions, though, failed to include Universal Coverage as the rational and logical solution to this "sick care," as he called it.

All of us are potential patients, and all of us believe in freedom. None of us should be denied the choice or the autonomy of health decisions. None of us should be exposed to the humiliation of preauthorization, precertification or the need for referral from a gatekeeper. But with all these privileges come the necessary responsibilities.

It is in the best interest of anybody who sells a product or a service to cater to the consumer. But, this shouldn't be the case when it comes to health care. In fact, the word "consumer" shouldn't be used to characterize our patients. I have already made it clear that this word has transformed the patient who basically requires alleviation of his ailment into a consumer who is conditioned to demand unnecessary products and services. Besides, the issue here is not a product, but the very facts of life and death. We should pamper the patient when he gets sick, but before that, we should demand responsibility from him. And as we follow the recommendation of the maintenance manual of our cars - or else we pay for expensive repairs – we should do the same with our health.

It is a fact that prevention is better, and cheaper, than cure. Patients should bear their share of the responsibility by stopping smoking, eating balanced and healthy diets, exercise regularly, avoid drugs and alcohol and become civil to, rather than kill, each other. All these are social issues and should be handled as such and not in a health care bill.

It is also a fact that treating ailments in their early stages is more effective and less costly than waiting for them to evolve into more chronic and disabling diseases that are more difficult to treat and much more expensive to cure. Yearly check ups and conscientious taking of the prescribed drugs are prerequisites to that effect.

We as individuals have to assume the responsibility of our civilized social contract. We are supposed not to litter, steal, kill or infringe on the freedoms of each other. It should not be less desirable to avoid unhealthy habits and disease producing life styles. Of course we can't, and we shouldn't, enforce specific ways of life, no matter how much desirable they are, but we can educate and encourage healthy behaviors. In fact we accomplished that when the number of smokers decreased following our campaign to reduce smoking

Society has an obligation to improve the environment, ensure a healthy supply of food and water, support research to enhance our health, reduce the incidence of accidents and control firearms besides combating other things that contribute to ill health and add cost to our health care system. Individually and collectively, all of us should share this responsibility.

If patients are unavoidable, doctors become the necessary evil we have to contend with. They stand out as the trustees of our health. They are also the determining force in delivering the care we need and the way we spend our health care dollars. Patients cannot diagnose their illness, nor can they write prescriptions, order MRI's or do surgery. It is the doctor's job to do all of that. A doctor's visit might cost us tens of dollars, but doctor's decisions might cost us hundreds and even thousands of dollars for prescription drugs, X rays and scanning, hospitalization and surgery. I admit that most of the time all of that is necessary, but as I have illustrated, sometimes not all of the doctors' interferences are necessary or of a proven value.

In any case, doctors' fees are only a fraction of our total cost - what goes into the doctors' pockets, as inflated as it is, is not the problem. The cost of doctors' decisions is the problem. However, we as a society must come up with the entire expense that might not only benefit the doctors financially but also might bankrupt us eventually.

As hard as I tried to expose the greed in some of our doctors, I have to make it clear here that the majority of our doctors are honorable professionals who are trying to make an honest living despite the presence of bad apples in their midst. Unfortunately, they have to behave at the same time as business people who are burdened with inflated overhead. They spend long years and expense on undergraduate and graduate education. They also spend extra years in training as interns, residents or fellows. Their working hours are long, and their responsibilities are tremendous. There is no doubt that they should be compensated adequately.

We have to reflect here, in passing, on the salaries of the professional athletes and the income of movie stars. If we value our health as much as we do our entertainment, we should pay our doctors accordingly. This leaves us with the question of how much is adequate and equitable in the case of doctors. As it stands now, 17% of our health care expenditure goes into doctors' pockets. With this much money, we can surely compensate each one of them, even if we have to put them on salaries that are proportional to their individual performance and productivity.

If we compensate doctors well, give them the freedom to compete, reduce their overhead and give them full autonomy, it becomes only proper to hold them accountable for their actions. We already have databases that were generated by Medicare and the private insurance companies. We can expand that into a national database to monitor and evaluate the performance of our doctors.

The privacy issue can be regulated and guaranteed as we did with our defense secrets. Actually, this privacy issue is more of a problem in the for-profit market where profiles on doctors and patients are traded as public commodities. The government is the only power that can guarantee our privacy. In fact, the Privacy Act of 1974 restrains the federal government, while corporate America has no such restraint. The head of our government, Richard Nixon, was impeached when, under his watch, the privacy of the opposing party was violated. This safeguard disappears in the case of the free market. Corporate America establishes profiles on our habits, the foods we eat, the places we go, the music we listen to, the clothes we wear and even the way we think, and they use all this private information to target us with their advertising and telemarketing with no fear of prosecution. It is clearly evident that we can enforce protection of our privacy much more easily with one government bureaucracy than with thousands of profit-seeking and fiercely competing entities.

Keep the malpractice threat but reform the tort laws to make it easier for the injured to be compensated quickly and fairly. (I discussed this subject in a previous chapter.)

We come now to the ideal payer. There is no doubt that the government, and only the government, should be the ideal payer. The government collects taxes, has the power to legislate and enforce any system we choose, and has the resources to manage an excess of a trillion dollar we spend on our health care. The government can save us over 30% of this money that is presently wasted on private administrative cost and equally as much that's stolen by fraudulent parasites and greedy and abusive behavior. Our democratic system can work in our favor to ensure that our government does the job efficiently and with less cost.

Fouad B. Michael, M.D.

A single payer system administered by the government and financed by income tax is the only practical and ideal solution. It is true that each country has its own social structure and demographics, and that a system that works for one country might not work for another. No system is perfect but we should be wise enough to learn from other countries' experiences. We should correctly start with something of proven merits and develop it as we proceed to the desired perfection. We actually have such a system, though limited in scope. It is called Medicare. This is not a welfare program; it is in fact paid for by our taxes when we are young, working and relatively healthy. It is administered by the government with only 3% of its budget going to administrative cost compared to 30% in case of the private insurance system. We don't have to reinvent the wheel. If all of us are included in Medicare, the resulting wider pool of healthy contributors would infuse much more money in it, enough o care for all of us when we happen to get sick.

Recent media sensational depiction of individual cases of less than perfect care distorts the accomplishments of the European and the Canadian systems. During the frenzy of obstructionist propaganda in the nineties, a front-page picture in the *New York Times* of a Canadian woman accompanied a report on the supposed deficiencies of the Canadian system. The picture showed an overweight woman on a stretcher in a hospital

144

corridor eating her breakfast. The report dramatized the 'sad' fact that this woman had been waiting for 5 years to get her coronary bypass surgery. We should rightfully wonder, if she had already survived 5 years without surgery, may be the surgery wasn't necessary to begin with, or at least it was of questionable value.

Another front-page article in the same newspaper, lamented the suffering of a British cancer patient who was denied a cancer drug that would have had extended her life a few more months. The article, though, didn't mention that this drug would have made the extra months not worth living because of the severe and devastating side effects it produces. Unfortunately, "death panels" and other misinformation and distortions were added to the debate in 2009. More pictures and stories like that have been used since then to obstruct any meaningful health care reform.

Dr. Melvin Konner, who holds Ph.D. and M.D. degrees from Harvard University and is a Professor of Anthropology and Associate Professor of Psychiatry and Neurology at Emory University, in his book, *Medicine at the Crossroads,* questioned the claim that America has the best health care system in the world:

> It can't be that we have the greatest longevity, many European
> countries have longer-lived people than we do, and some
> groups in our society do not even meet the standards of the

145

developing world in longevity: men in Harlem have lower life expectancies than men in Bangladesh. It can't be that we have the best prenatal care, since we have made no organized effort and so have a rate of preventable premature birth that is higher than in other countries.

It can't be infant mortality, where we are twenty-third lowest. It can't be child health, since children are far over-represented among the uninsured, and since we have one of the largest proportions of non-immunized children of any industrialized country...It certainly cannot be fairness, since more than 35 million people are uninsured...And it cannot be efficiency, since costs are out of control.

In fact, the World Health Organization (WHO) in its *World Health Report 2000,* showed that European health care systems are generally performing best and that the United States is lagging behind – the five top nations for health care parameters were France, Italy, San Marino, Andora and Malta (all have some form of a national health care system), and the U.S. ranked 37 out of a total of 191 nations that are members of WHO.

A more convincing reason for the obvious value of universal health care was the ranking of China as the number 188 when the Chinese people are now paying for virtually all their care out of pocket. Compare this to its ranking as the 144th just a decade earlier when it had a public health care system.

Another surprise, but an encouraging one, is that Oman, a small country on the Persian Gulf, ranked number 8 in recent survey when only in the 1970's it had a very high infant mortality, and that this high ranking was accomplished with a relatively small budget for health care, as small as one-tenth of that of the U.S.

It is necessary to understand in this regard that there is a difference between health care and medical care as I had alluded to above. Health care is measured by life expectancy, infant mortality, accessibility and other universal bench marks, which are better accomplished by at least 36 countries than us.

Yes, we can transplant more hearts and livers, do more surgeries that border on the miraculous, churn out more MRI's and keep our terminally-ill patients unnecessarily alive longer than any other country. This is medical care at its best, but it is only available to some of our patients and it is not the health care we're talking about. This best medical care is glamorous, but it is individualistic, exclusionary, non-sustainable and way too much expensive. Realistically, we can't afford it anymore.

How is it that we ranked that low in health care among the industrialized nations when we have the best medical care and the highest per-capita expenditure?

What Joseph Califano wrote in his book, *Radical Surgery,* explains some of the reasons for this paradox. "[W]e waste some $250 billion. We are buying billions in bureaucratic waste…We are buying billions in fraud and abuse…[A]s much as $100 billion a year is lost through fraud and abuse, including padded bills, charges for tests and procedures never performed, and double billing." (These figures are much higher if they are adjusted to inflation)

Using Califano's previous conclusion in this regard, I have to add that fragmentation inherent in giving over a trillion dollar to over 1'500 insurance companies to manage our health care, and their motive to make profit, are other reason for this paradox.

The government with, our consent and cooperation and with its overreaching power can cut down on fraud and abuse. Who else has the machinery and the reach to punish the greedy doctors and eliminate the parasitic profiteering from health care?

The government can insure better environment through regulation to control pollutants and other poisons that are detrimental to our health.

Who else can prevent factories from one state from spewing pollutants that fall as acid rain on another state?

The government can support research for new drugs and procedures much more effectively, and far less costly, than the for-profit industries.

The government is bound by our laws to protect our privacy, build safer roads, require safer cars and industrial products to minimize accidents, control firearms so we don't kill each other, help educate our citizens about health hazards like smoking, alcohol and drugs.

The government has been trying to accomplish all that with variable success. In fact, we have no other choice but to trust our government to manage our health care. All we need is to simplify the laws to decrease the unnecessary and expensive bureaucracies.

Two books are a must read for every citizen of this country especially for every politician, news reporter and pundit who try to denigrate any universal health care system.

The first book is titled *Health Care & Reform in Industrialized Countries,* published by Pennsylvania State University and edited by Marshall W. Raffel. It presents, without bias, the actual faces of the national health care systems in Canada, Western Europe and Japan.

The idea of national health care is not new. It has been in practice for over half a century. How illogical of us to ignore these experiences and keep on trying other things. Every surgeon knows that it is much easier to perform an operation from scratch than to correct a botched one. National health care has been proven by other countries to be the best care available. There is no more need for further experimentation.

The second book is *Universal Health Care, What the United States Can Learn From The Canadian Experience*, written by Pat and Hugh Armstrong with Claudia Fagen, M.D., and published by The New Press, New York.

I would like to quote some sentences from this valuable book to illustrate the beauty of the Canadian system. "…[I]t accomplishes five basic principles: comprehensiveness, universality, portability, accessibility through public administration." And it had done that "with a health act that took only 13 pages to write."

"Doctors in Canada keep their autonomy and are paid on the fee-for-service schedule negotiated by their societies. They can work wherever they want, practice whatever they decide and deal with only one payer with minimum paper work or regulations.

"Patients can see any doctor they choose, go to any hospital they prefer, get the care they need across provinces' boundaries and even outside their country's boundaries. No bills submitted and no questions asked."

Furthermore, this book makes it clear that the feared abuse of free care by patients proved not to be a problem; the number of patients' visits to doctors never increased. The waiting lines for elective, and only elective, surgery or MRI do not compare to our de facto rationing due to lack of insurance or inadequate insurance.

A government run single payer system funded by taxes and governed by the fewest rules and regulations possible is clearly the best we can strive for. We already have such a system in Medicare, though limited in scope as I have made it clear, and our seniors swear by it. It can be expanded to cover all of us. Anything else is bound to fail.

Epilogue

I came to America as an immigrant well prepared to follow in the footsteps of the pioneers of this great country. Although I found no frontiers to discover, no territories to conquer and no wars to fight, I had the will to serve. I believe that I have served my patients as best as I could in the noble profession I chose.

I came to America believing in the supremacy of democracy and the ideals of social justice, hard work and human dignity. My beliefs were strengthened by my encounters with the patients I cared for and the great doctors I worked with.

I came to America with the yearning to be free. But I learned that true freedom is gained by assuming the required responsibilities by both the individual and society as a whole. I was still a student in medical school when Kennedy said, "ask not what your country can do for you but what you can do for your country." How appropriate this sentence is for our time and for all time.

I also learned that the sick are never free, that the abuse, the fraud and the waste can never be responsible acts, and that a democratic government is never too big to defy control by its own people.

When I retired from the practice of medicine at the age 62, my colleagues envied me. Most of them declared that they would do the same if they could. It is a fact that doctors are retiring at a younger age, and the ones who can't are currently working under severe stressful conditions that would undoubtedly affect their performance to the detriment of their patients. Doctors now talk to each other less about how to manage their patients' problems and more on how to survive.

The real danger, however, is the drop in the applicants for medical schools. Worse still is the drop in the quality of those who apply. This is not what we want for our future doctors. Our brightest are seeking other more lucrative professions. We are not only losing the experienced doctors early, but we are also damaging the lifeline that supplies them. The danger might not be around the corner yet, but it is certainly looming in the near future.

The change of the medical profession from a calling to a business is even more damaging. Making money, not proper patient care, is becoming the pressing concern of the new medical environment. The old-time dedicated doctor is giving way to the new businessman. And all of us would ultimately pay a high price for this change.

Our patients have been abused and fooled enough. It is time to save them from the abuses of the free market health care, and give them the compassionate care of a national health care system. After all, they are the ones who pay the cost, and what they currently pay is more than enough to buy the best health care they need, if we eliminate the waste, the parasites, the abuse, the fraud and the greed.

My American dream, and yours, would not be complete unless this wonderful country adopts the health care system that takes care of all of us in sickness and in health.

About the Author

Fouad B. Michael, M.D. was born in Palestine (now Israel) to Egyptian parents. He received his M.D. degree from Cairo University, Egypt, in 1961 and completed his internships and residencies both in Egypt and the United States. He worked as an Otolaryngologist (Ear Nose and Throat specialist) in Rockville Centre, N.Y. In addition to his private practice, he taught at the New York Eye and Ear Infirmary in New York City.

After an early retirement in January 2000, he moved to Charlottesville, Virginia, where he is currently living with his wife and pursuing his interests in classical music, sculpture, reading and writing. All his published works are on health care reform. Several of his essays were included in medical publications and a number of his letters-to-the-editor on this subject appeared in daily newspapers. He is in the process of publishing a novel, Kantara, a volume of short stories and one of poetry.